Truth and Meaning

By the same author:

God, the Family and Democracy

Essays in Human Relations

TRUTH AND MEANING

by

David Greenwood

Foreword by Herbert L. Searles,
Professor of Philosophy, University of Southern California

PHILOSOPHICAL LIBRARY
NEW YORK

Copyright, 1957, by

PHILOSOPHICAL LIBRARY, INC.

15 East 40th Street, New York 16, N.Y.

PRINTED IN THE UNITED STATES OF AMERICA

To the Members of the Los Angeles
Branch of the Oxford Society, whom
I have had the privilege of serving as
their Secretary.

τῷ σοφῷ ξένον οὐδέν·

—Antisthenes.

Foreword

PROFESSOR GREENWOOD has written a provocative book in the highly controversial areas of contemporary logic, semiotic and epistemology. He moves freely and penetratingly among the concepts and problems in these fields and is at home with his authorities, albeit perhaps with too ready an assumption that his reader is equally conversant with the sources. Familiarity with the contemporary literature in logic and semantics is a necessary condition of a complete grasp of the many technical arguments.

Professor Greenwood exhibits skill in placing his finger upon the most controversial issues in the various areas covered, from Tarski's semantical definition of truth, to the conflict between the apriorist and the frequentist in probability theory, and the analytic versus the synthetic interpretation of mathematics.

The key to the clarification of the semantical definition of truth is found in the essential logical strength and richness of the metalanguage. Problems of meaning in natural languages revolve around the analysis of intension, which is taken to be an empirical hypothesis. The ambiguity of "completeness" in the sentential calculus is due to the failure to distinquish clearly between syntactical and semantical concepts. The problem of mathematical definition is largely due to the differing interpretations of mathematics. On the whole Professor Greenwood tends to side with Kant over against the purely analytic and linguistic interpretation of mathematics, but anticipates a synthesis of the two viewpoints in the future.

In a final chapter on "The Pragmatic Theory of Truth" the discussion is rounded out and a semi-popular note is lent to the conclusion. From Peirce to Dewey the theory is surveyed in broad strokes and with sympathetic insight into the essential meaning of the pragmatic account of meaning and truth. Against the many misunderstandings extant the Pragmatists are defended.

The author's position is frequently proposed independently of the many conflicting positions cited, and again he takes sides with one or more disputants in preference to others. Fortunately for us it is not necessary in this brief Foreword to try to adjudicate the conflicting views argued. This pleasant task is bequeathed to the interested reader.

University of Southern California   HERBERT L. SEARLES

Table of Contents

Preface

THIS volume contains six essays which were written at various times during the past four years and are here presented under one cover. It is sincerely hoped that in this way they may be of some service to philosophers, scientists and social scientists interested in the logical and methodological foundations of their subject.

I have not drawn any distinction between logic in general and any special "logic of empirical sciences," since I am inclined to doubt if any such division exists. Logical concepts and methods have not so far found fruitful applications in the methodology of empirical sciences. I suspect that this paucity of logical applications arises from the fact that, for the purpose of an adequate methodological treatment, empirical sciences have to be considered not only as systems of asserted statements arranged according to rigorous rules, but also as complexes consisting partly of such statements and partly of human activities. The methodology of the empirical sciences can hardly boast of definite achievements comparable to those of the sciences themselves, and even the clarification of basic methodological concepts is in a comparatively nebulous state. Nevertheless, the prospects of achievement in the future seem promising.

My gratitude is due to many thinkers for their interest: Lord Russell, Rudolph Carnap and the late Hans Reichenbach in particular. Where I have differed from these authorities, I trust that my criticisms have been helpful and constructive rather than merely iconoclastic. There is surely no virtue in criticism which has nothing substantial to contribute in building up a better synthesis than that already existing.

I also wish to thank Professor Donald Piatt of the University of California at Los Angeles for his careful criticism of an early draft of "The Pragmatic Theory of Truth," and Professor Herbert Searles of the University of Southern California for the Foreword. My sincere indebtedness to other authorities is too great to permit of detailed acknowledgement.

Beverly Hills, California   DAVID GREENWOOD

Truth and Meaning

Truth and Metalanguage

THE concise definition of truth and falsehood provided by Tarski deserves more general recognition than has hitherto been accorded it. The *ipsissima verba* are these:

"A sentence is true if it is satisfied by all objects, and false otherwise."[1]

I believe that one can hold Tarski's view without abandoning any previously held epistemological attitude. The semantical concept of truth is completely neutral towards other definitions, realist, idealist, empiricist, metaphysical or any other, and is best arrived at by the use of other semantic notions, e.g. designation, satisfaction and definition. But while these notions express relations between certain expressions and the objects referred to by these expressions, truth, in terms of semantics, expresses a property or denotes a class of sentences. In this respect the problem of defining truth is very closely allied to the general problem of erecting the foundations of theoretical semantics.

Before the definition of any semantical concept can be given, it is first of all necessary to specify the formal structure of the language to be used. The general conditions under which the structure of a language is exactly specified are these:

1. The class of those words and expressions which are to be considered meaningful must be characterized unambiguously.
2. All undefined words (primitive terms) must be indicated.

3. All defined terms should be given rules of definition.
4. Criteria should be given for distinguishing within the class of expressions those under the category of sentences.
5. The conditions under which a sentence of the language can be asserted must be formulated. This involves indicating all axioms (primitive sentences) and providing rules of proof for deducing new asserted sentences from previously asserted sentences.

Since the use of semantically closed languages involves inconsistencies,[2] the discussion of truth is best confined to object-language and metalanguage. The formal relations between object-language and metalanguage rest largely on the question of whether the metalanguage is essentially richer than the object-language or not. With regard to languages based on the logical theory of types, the condition for the metalanguage to be essentially richer than the object-language is that it should include variables of a higher logical type than those of the object-language. Essential richness, as Tarski has shown,[3] is not only necessary, but sufficient for the satisfactory definition of truth.

The definition itself is most easily obtained from the notion of satisfaction, or a relation between arbitrary objects and sentential functions. In defining the notion of a sentential function recourse is most frequently made to recursive procedure. This may consist in forming the logical conjunction or disjunction of two given functions. Thus a sentence may be defined as a sentential function containing no free variables. By the same procedure, a general definition of satisfaction may be formulated. Indication is first given as to which objects satisfy the simplest sentential functions and then which conditions enable given objects to satisfy a compound function. This assumes, of course, that it is already known which objects satisfy the simpler functions from which the compound one has been constructed. Thus given numbers satisfy the logical disjunction "x is greater than y or x is equal to y" if they satisfy at least one of the functions "x is greater than y" or "x is equal to y."

The definition of satisfaction, it will be noticed, applies automatically also to sentences, i.e. special sentential functions which contain no free variables. Thus a sentence is either satisfied by all objects or no objects, and these are the only two possible cases. Hence follows the definition of truth and falsehood already given. A clearer idea of the involvement of the essential richness of the metalanguage is provided by three methods:

1. Admission of the recursive definition of the notion of satisfaction—a form of definition which is not admitted to the object-language.
2. Introduction into the metalanguage of variables of a higher logical type than those which occur in the object-language.
3. Assumption axiomatically in the metalanguage of the existence of classes that are more comprehensive than all those whose existence can be established in the object-language.[4]

These last two procedures make it possible to eliminate all recursive definitions and to replace them by normal, explicit definitions.

As well as being formally correct, Tarski's definition also seems materially adequate in the sense that it implies all equivalences of the form:

$$\text{X is true, if and only if, p.}$$

The conditions for the material adequacy of the definition determine uniquely the extension of the term "true," and therefore every definition of truth which is materially adequate would of necessity be equivalent to that constructed.

From the semantic definition of truth various results can be deduced applicable to other semantic notions, e.g. designation, definition, consequence, synonymity and meaning. Underlying all these is the distinction between the object-language and the metalanguage. In every case the necessary and sufficient condition for a satisfactory definition of the notion involved is the essential richness of the metalanguage. The construction of metalanguages, then, is of fundamental importance to all semantical notions.

The metalanguage M, I presuppose, may be analysed by the method of extension and intension. A sentence is extensional if its extension is a function of the extension of the designator. A sentence is intensional if its intension is a function of the intension of the designator. This procedure avoids the basic weaknesses of the name-relation method which fails to distinguish between meaning and application and ultimately involves the user in the antinomy of the name-relation. Carnap[5] clearly shows that the various methods of keeping the name-relation but avoiding the antinomy lead to two further problems: the development of great complications in the language structure, and serious restrictions in the use of language or in the application of the semantical method.

One apparent difficulty of M is that it implies a duplication of entities, using different expressions for classes and properties. It is possible, however, to construct a metalanguage M^1 which, while being neutral, preserves all previous distinctions in different formulations. Any discussion of M and M^1 has to take place in a metametalanguage MM. One can thus use terms such as "class," "property," "extension" and "intension" in MM, though these cannot, of course, occur in M^1 itself. It is then reasonable to say that the extension of "Blue" in M^1 is the class "Blue," and the intension of "Blue" in M^1 is the property "Blue." Similarly, the extension of "Goethe" in M^1 is the individual Goethe, whilst the intension of "Goethe" in M^1 is the individual concept "Goethe." The last two examples have been in MM, for without reference to the metametalanguage, the terms "Blue" and "Goethe" in M^1 are neutral.

A problem arises in connection with the translation of identity sentences into M^1 in view of the fact that classes and properties have different identity conditions. Three sentences will provide an example:

    1. The class Orator is the same as the class Speaker.

2. The property Orator is not the same as the property Speaker.

3. The property Orator is the same as the property Demagogue.

In the sentences Nos. 1 and 2 a contradiction would result from the omission of the words "class" and "property." A neutral formulation cannot speak about identity, since identity is different for extensions and intensions. It is therefore not permissible to use identity phrases (e.g. "is the same as") in M^1.

The concept of equivalence and L-equivalence, as developed by Carnap,[6] seems to be one solution to this problem. If two designators are equivalent in a symbolic language system S_1, their extensions are identical and their intensions are equivalent. If two designators are L- equivalent in S_1, their intensions are identical or L- equivalent. Identity of extensions thus coincides with equivalence of intensions, and identity of intensions coincides with the L- equivalence of intensions. The terms "equivalent" and "L-equivalent" can be used, without any undue straining of connotation, in connection with neutral phrases instead of phrases for intensions. By this method a sentence stating identity of extensions is best translated into M^1 as a sentence stating equivalence of neutral entities, whilst a sentence stating identity of intensions is translated into M^1 as a sentence stating L- equivalence of neutral entities. The translation of the three sentences above will then appear as:

1. Orator is equivalent to Speaker.
2. Orator is not L- equivalent to Speaker.
3. Orator is L- equivalent to Demagogue.

The last three sentences, which belong to the non-semantical, non-semiotic part of M^1, should be differentiated from the following three, which are semantical sentences in MM dealing with certain predications in M^1, the predicators being enclosed in quotation marks:

1. "Orator" is equivalent to "Speaker" in M^1.

2. "Orator" is not L- equivalent to "Speaker" in M^1.
3. "Orator" is L- equivalent to "Demagogue" in M^1.

The translation of atomic sentences into M^1 is a comparatively simple procedure. Thus, as a translation of 'Pg' in M^1, the simplest translation in M to take is "Goethe is a poet." The neutral translation in M^1 replaces the non-neutral sentences in M:

1. Goethe has the property Poet.
2. Goethe belongs to the class Poet.

It also replaces the two non-neutral phrases: "The truth value that Goethe is a poet" and "the proposition that Goethe is a poet" in M.

Additional problems arise when the sentence "Goethe is a poet" occurs as a grammatical object or in the position of a subordinate clause. Thus the two sentences:

1. "Goethe is a poet," said the lecturer emphatically.
2. Nobody seriously denies that Goethe is a poet.

both involve difficulties which embrace syntactical rather than semantical laws. The same applies to fictitious and nonsensical designators, i.e. those which do not in fact have and those which could not conceivably have extensions. I take it that those are exceptions to the now well founded semantical law that every designator has both an intension and an extension. As a fictitious designator does not and a nonsensical designator cannot apply to anything, it is clear that the question of whether a designator does apply to anything cannot arise until after its meaning, if it has any, is known.

The question now arises of whether M^1 has the same essential richness as M. Thus Quine,[7] basing himself on the usual method of the name-relation, doubted by implication whether any designators in a metalanguage could be described as neutral. The word "Poet" in M^1 must then mean either "the class Poet" or "the property Poet" or else be ambiguous.

I believe that Quine's objection can be met with the concept of what I shall call Unsymmetrical Neutrality. A semantical rule for any sign stands primarily for its intension, and only secondarily, with the help of relevant facts, for its extension. A designator may therefore be regarded, in a sense, as a name of its own intension. With reference to intensional languages like M^1, it is better to apply the name to a designator's intension rather than to its extension. The intension, after all, is what is actually conveyed by the designator from the speaker to the listener. The extension relates to the location of application of the designator, so that the listener can only determine it with the help of factual knowledge in addition to his understanding of the designator. In this respect, I agree that the connotation of a designator is nearer to its intension than to its extension. This is what I mean by the concept of Unsymmetrical Neutrality.

It does not follow that M^1 is less rich than M because it does not contain the phrase "the class Poet." Whatever is said in M with the help of this phrase is immediately translatable into M^1 with the help of "Poet." Indeed, in all sentences, except those in the category of identity sentences, class expressions (e.g. "the class Poet") and property expressions (e.g. "the property Poet") are translated by the corresponding neutral expressions (e.g. "Poet"). A sentence stating identity of classes is translated into a sentence stating the equivalence of the corresponding neutral entities and a sentence stating the L- equivalence of the corresponding neutral entities. The fact that the neutrality of designators in M^1 is not symmetrical does not invalidate these general laws.

The whole semantics of any system S_1 can be translated from M into M^1. Two sentences, both in M, will help to explain the procedure:

1. The extension of 'P' in S_1 is the class Poet.
2. The intension of 'P' in S_1 is the property Poet.

The first sentence indicates that the relation of extension holds between the class Poet and the predicator 'P' (in S_1) and the second sentence indicates that the relation of intension holds between the property Poet and the predicator 'P' (in S_1). In order to obtain neutral formulations in M^1 referring to the neutral entity Poet without reference to class and property, relations must be utilized which hold between the neutral entity Poet and the predicator 'P.' These relations must, of course, be neither the relation of extension nor that of intension, though they should be similar to both of them.

The relations which seem suitable are two in number, and these I propose to call designation and L- designation.[8] Then instead of the last two sentences on the class Poet and the property Poet in M, a rule of designation for the system S_1 may be formulated in M^1:

'P' designates Poet.

This sentence indicates an extensional relationship, so that the word 'Poet' is interchangeable with any predicator which is equivalent to 'Poet' in M^1.

In the same way that it seems unnecessary for symbolic systems to use different variables for classes and for properties, so the phrases "for every class" and "for every property" in M seem to entail useless duplication. In M^1 they may be replaced by a neutral variable whose value-intensions are properties and whose value-extensions are classes. If this neutral variable is called 'n,' the further result may be given[9]:

For every n, if n is equivalent to Poet, then 'P' designates n in S_1.

This may reasonably be regarded as a translation of the first sentence:

The extension of 'P' in S_1 is the class Poet.

The concept of L- designation, the second relation, is similar. The general rule is this:

For every n, if n is L-equivalent to Poet, then 'P' L- designates n in S_1.

This, in its turn, may reasonably be regarded as a translation of the second sentence:

The intension of 'P' in S_1 is the property Poet.

So far it has been maintained that semantical sentences in M stating the extensions or intensions of predicators can be translated into neutral formulations in M^1. The same procedures may be applied analogously to other types of designators. Individual expressions and sentences in S_1 can be similarly translated. Thus the translation of this sentence in M:

"The extension of 'a' is the individual Aquinas."

may be either or both of these:

1. 'a' designates Aquinas.
2. For every n, if n is equivalent to Aquinas, then 'a' designates n.

Similarly the translation of this sentence in M:

"The intension of 'a' is the individual concept Aquinas."

may be either or both of these:

1. 'a' L- designates Aquinas.
2. For every n, if n is L- equivalent to Aquinas, then 'a' L- designates n.

The translation of this sentence in M:

"The extension of the sentence 'Pg' in S_1 is the truth value that Goethe is a poet, which happens to be the truth."

may be either or both of these:

1. 'Pg' designates that Goethe is a poet. (The introduction of a that-clause for the neutral formation is permissible and necessary in English as it lacks other grammatical procedures for avoiding the introduction of a subordinate clause, cf. the accusative-infinitive construction in Latin.)

2. For every n, if n is equivalent to (the fact) that Goethe is a poet, then 'Pg' designates n.

Similarly the translation of this sentence in M:

"The intension of the sentence 'Pg' in S_1 is the proposition that Goethe is a poet."

may be either or both of these:

1. 'Pg' L- designates that Goethe is a poet.
2. For every n, if n is L- equivalent to (the fact) that Goethe is a poet, then 'Pg' L- designates n.

It would seem, then, that S_1 or any other semantical system may be translated from M to M^1. The question of which to use is largely a matter of choice, but the neutral formulation seems preferable for cases such as the development of the definition of semantical truth where the metalanguage has to be constructed on a strict systematized basis, in symbolic languages and in words whose use is governed by explicit rules. The rigid structure of M^1 allows its further division into submetalanguages M^e, M^1, M^s. It seems plausible that a complete semantical description of a system, e.g. S_2 can be formulated in an extensional metalanguage provided that a clear differentiation is made between the various areas of the vocabulary of the original metalanguage. Thus the divisions of the vocabulary of the metalanguage M would seem to be:

1. The logical vocabulary, containing logical constants and general variables.
2. The syntactical vocabulary, containing names of the signs in the object language L, a notation for concatenation and syntactical variables.
3. The non-semiotical vocabulary, containing descriptive constants referring to non-linguistic entities.
4. The semantical vocabulary, containing the semantical terms defined on the basis of the other three parts.

These divisions seem basic to metalanguage structure in general;

it is only surprising that philosophers, with notable exceptions, have done so little work in the past on the analysis of metalanguage.

My general conception of semantical truth and the construction of metalanguages as an aid in its clarification rests to a large extent on the theories of Frege, Tarski, Russell and Carnap. However much these theorists differ, they all agree in general that discussions of the term "truth" should involve, at some point or another, the question of the relation of signs to things. Thus a sign combination such as "Fido" designates 'A' is an instance of a semantical sentence. Here "Fido" denotes 'Fido' (i.e. the sign or the sign vehicle and not a non-linguistic object), while 'A' is an indexical sign of some object, (e.g. the word 'that' used in connection with some directive gesture). "Fido" is thus a term in the metalanguage denoting the sign 'Fido' in the object language; 'A' is a term in the thing-language denoting a thing. Designation, then, implies a relation between a sign and an object.

Since this whole synthesis has been attacked from several quarters, it would be well to probe the foundations more deeply to ascertain if the structure is secure. It is undeniable that Frege, like Russell, inherited the traditional belief, which ultimately stems from the works of J. S. Mill, that to ask:

What does the expression "E" mean?

is tantamount to saying:

What does "E" stand in the relationship in which "Fido" stands to Fido?

Thus the significance of any expression is the thing, process, person or entity of which the expression is the proper name. This theory may result from the fact that proper names are visible or audible things, and are frequently attached in a familiar way to visible and audible things such as human beings, cities, rivers, etc. This procedure is then applied to expressions which are not proper names and the meanings of the expression is then taken as being analogous to the relationship between the extra-linguistic correlate, dog, and his name, Fido.

The use of the assimilation of proper names as expressions in M and M¹ (as, following Frege, I have used earlier in this paper) has been condemned by Ryle on many occasions, both in published work and in unpublished lectures at Oxford.[10] Nobody ever asks the meaning of Robinson Crusoe, he argues, still less who is the meaning of Robinson Crusoe. We do not say that the river Mississippi has a meaning *ex vi termini*. A man may be described as "the person called 'Goethe,' " but not as "the meaning of 'Goethe.' " There are some cases in which Frege's basic procedure will not work in English at all, e.g. in the sentence

"Nijni Novgorod is in Russia."

Here Ryle stipulates that it is not clear whether this sentence contains three, four or five English words.

These are serious criticisms, but I do not believe they are unanswerable. First of all, even the most staunch supporters of the "Fido"—Fido principle have admitted its occasional fallibility. Frege pointed out that the phrases "the evening star" and "the morning star" do not have the same sense (*Sinn*), even if they happen to denote (*bedeuten*) the same planet. One can understand the meaning of the expression "the first Emperor of the United States" even though it patently does not apply to anyone. This concession of Frege deserves more attention than it has received, for by extending its application it can cover all single entities with more than one proper name. In those cases one really is arguing as to the meaning of the proper name as a single expression. Furthermore, Ryle's contention that nobody asks the meaning of Robinson Crusoe would imply that nobody appreciates the difference between:

1. The man on a desert island to whom the name applies.
2. Any other person who, whether on a desert island or not, decides that he likes the name and proceeds to apply it to himself.

3. The manifestation of a particularly fine choice of two English names by the novelist Defoe.

4. The etymological meaning—a man by the surname of Crusoe whose given name implies that he, or a man who bore the name before him, was the son of Robin.

5. The combination in two words of the fourteen English letters R-O-B-I-N-S-O-N C-R-U-S-O-E.

6. The use of Robinson Crusoe in a tautologous example:

$$\text{Robinson Crusoe} = \text{Robinson Crusoe.}$$

This contention is too sweeping. Frege's exception can also be extended to cover these meanings.

Frege also modified the "Fido"—Fido principle in another way. The traditional doctrine of terms required the analysis of proposition-expressing sentences into two or three terms, all supposed to be correlated with entities in the "Fido"—Fido way. But a sentence must include some syncategorematic words, i.e. expressions which are not terms, such as "is," "if," "a," etc. These words are not meaningless though they are not names, as all categorematic words were erroneously supposed to be. It is true that the use of some languages (e.g. Latin) or of special English grammatical constructions sometimes alleviates the necessity of using syncategorematic words, but this does not help to deal with the situations where they are necessary. Taken by themselves they are regarded as incomplete without collocations with other expressions, in contradistinction to categorematic words which are non-auxiliary and syntactically complete without collocations. On this basis, "Fido" or "the first Emperor of the United States" are both meaningful expressions even when taken by themselves *in vacuo.*

The doctrine of incomplete symbols, as expounded by Russell, was a first attempt to shift certain expressions from the categorematic to the syncategorematic group. It was not completely successful because it assumed that there still existed some categorematic expressions which would brook being said *sans phrase.* To call an expression "incomplete" was mistakenly assumed to be saying that it did not function like a name, thus setting the standard of syntactical completeness by names rather than by sentences. It is saying, in effect, that it is only a fragment of a range of possible sentences. Thus proper names are as incomplete as any other sentence-fragments, with the possible exceptions of some special vocative uses.

For the sake of consistency, Frege then applied the modified "Fido"—Fido principle to expressions of all types with the exception of those which were indubitably syncategorematic. Thus he concluded that an indicative sentence both names an entity and has a sense (*Sinn*), or in other words it denotes a truth-value and connotes a proposition (*Gedanke*).

I have followed the usage of Carnap in further modifying the "Fido"—Fido principle and instead of using Frege's terms "names" and "predicates," I have differentiated between designators and predicators. I do not believe that this is a complete solution to the terminological problem. There is still some doubt in my own mind as to the extent of independence of meaning that expressions may possess under the general category of "designator." Contemporary usage does not appear completely consistent. But the further subdivisions of extension and intension seem to reduce some of the vagueness attached to the more traditional terminology.

That problems still remain to be solved in the general area of extension and intension in the metalanguage is made even more patent by the ambiguity which has always surrounded the word "all." I see two streams of argument as having existed amongst philosophers. Sometimes "all" means "every" and sometimes "any" and this difference led some philosophers, e.g. Joseph and Keynes, to assert that in the sentence "all men are mortal," the principal significance of the sentence is that it refers to men. The other stream of argument, as expounded in the work of Russell and others, was about the dual function of all categorematic words that are employable in the subject-place in subject-predicate sentences. Thus the sentence "all men are mortal" implies primarily that there cannot be any immortal men. Fundamentally this divergence of views is between classing "all men are mortal" as a categorical or a hypothetical sentence. The supporters of the categorical interpretation generally agree that the subject-term of the sentence must, *qua* subject-term, name or denote some men. The supporters of the hypothetical interpretation generally agree that the protasis of a hypothetical is not asserted as true, and that the whole hypothetical could be true even though it were actually false that any men existed. Thus the protasis does not name or denote any men.

The traditional debate over names and predicates involved the assumption that the two premises and the conclusion of any syllogism were isomorphous subject-predicate propositions and, out of respect for Barbara, took analogous propositions of the same bi-polar type, and used them as standard models. It was assumed that propositions, in general, were analysable into subject-term, copula, and predicate-term, the two end terms being interchangeable under certain conditions. Where the subject terms of such sentences are used mentioningly, the persons or things mentioned are the extensions which do seem to fit into the extension-intension scheme. I list a few below:

1. Propositions of fiction, where subject-terms are used only quasi-mentioningly.
2. Affirmative or negative existence-propositions.
3. Sentences of the "any S is P" type.

This still leaves the problems of non-bi-polar propositions and subject terms of bi-polar propositions used in a manner other than mentioningly. One does not wish to repeat the Frege-Meinong mistake of treating sentences as names, for this forced a whole group of sentences and sentence-fragments into a meaningful category which, by themselves, had no meaning at all. Thus "is mortal" is not a mentioning expression, and has no meaning *in vacuo*. As such, this fragment can have no extension or intension. These cases create special problems in metalanguage construction which philosophers are still a long way from settling.

Despite its drawbacks, which I feel are probably temporary, the method of extension and intension grapples with the problem, which the name-relation method by-passed, of the distinction between meaning and application. This led to the erroneous conception that an expression must be the name of exactly one of the two semantical factors involved, a conception which could only possibly lead to the name-relation antimony. Furthermore, the extension-intension method helps in the clarification of problems of the modalities with quantified variables. Its use in metalanguage construction would seem to be a significant contribution towards a fuller conception of semantical truth and ultimately of universal truth.

NOTES

1. Tarski, A.: "The Semantic Conception of Truth," *Philosophy and Phenomenological Research*, 4, 1944, p. 353. Reprinted in:
   (a) Linsky, L.: "Semantics and the Philosophy of Language," University of Illinois Press, 1952
   (b) Feigl, H. and Sellars, W.: "Readings in Philosophical Analysis," Appleton-Century, 1949.
2. Op. cit., p. 348.
3. Op. cit., p. 352.
4. Vide:
   Tarski, A.: "On Undecidable Statements in Enlarged Systems of Logic and the Concept of Truth," *Journal of Symbolic Logic*, Vol. IV, 1939, pp. 105–112.
5. Carnap, R.: "Meaning and Necessity," University of Chicago Press, 1947, pp. 96–136. The solutions of Frege, Quine, Church and Russell are sympathetically discussed but inevitably abandoned.
6. Based on the distinction between radical concepts and L- concepts in:
   Carnap, R.: "Introduction to Semantics." Harvard, 1942.
7. Quine, W. V.: "Notes on Existence and Necessity," *Journal of Philosophy*, XL (1943), pp. 113–127.
8. These terms are open to immediate objection as logicians themselves are by no means agreed as to the exact connotations of the word "designation." Thus Church's remark ("Carnap's Introduction to Semantics," *Philosophical Review*, LII, 1943, pp.

299–300), that the designation of a sentence is not a proposition but a truth-value seems to include what other logicians would categorise under the term "nominatum." I interpret "designatum" as generally equivalent to intension in M, and "L-designatum" as generally equivalent to intension in M^1.

9. Carnap ("Meaning and Necessity," pp. 160, 161), differentiates between variables for predicators of level one and degree one as value expressions, variables for individual expressions, and variables for sentences. All these receive different letters. Thus

'f,' 'g,' etc. = predicators of level one and degree one as value expressions,

'x,' 'y,' etc. = individual expressions,

'p,' 'q,' etc. = sentences.

One criticism of this system has been that it is not universally valid in as much as these three categories may overlap on occasions, e.g. the complete sentence used vocatively as the subject of a verb. Nevertheless I feel that it is most valuable once its limitations and exceptions have been clarified.

10. See, for example, the Discussion of "Meaning and Necessity" in *Philosophy*, Vol. 88, Jan. 1949, pp. 69–76.

Meaning in Natural Languages

IN attempting to analyse the meaning of any given expression, it is possible to distinguish between two operations, the first consisting of the understanding of the expression itself, and the second being more concerned with the factual situation referred to by the given expression. These two procedures are respectively the intensional and the extensional, the development of their theory being largely due to the work of Carnap and C. I. Lewis. I use the word 'intension' in the restricted sense of applying only to the cognitive or designative meaning component, and the analysis of this for a natural language I believe to be a sound scientific procedure. The assignment of an intension is an empirical hypothesis which can be tested by observing language behavior in exactly the same way as any other linguistic hypothesis.

This standpoint has been attacked by Quine[1] who, broadly speaking, takes the position that the assignment of an intension, on the foundation of the already determined extension, is largely a matter of choice and may be any of those properties which fit the given extension. Thus he writes:

"The finished lexicon is a case evidently of ex pede Herculem. But there is a difference. In projecting Hercules from the foot we risk error but we derive comfort from the fact that there is something to be wrong about. In the case of the lexicon, pending some definition of synonymy, we have no stating of the problem; we have nothing for the lexicographer to be right or wrong about."

In other words, pragmatical intension concepts are so vague and undetermined that they are hardly worth bothering about.

If this thesis were correct, I believe that it would be possible to make any number of statements purporting to be true which could not possibly have any logical veracity whatever, e.g. the two statements:

1. 'Mulier' is the Latin word for 'woman'
2. 'Mulier' is the Latin word for 'woman' or 'fairy.'

Since I take it that there are no fairies, the two intensions of the word 'mulier' have the same extension. If Quine is correct, there is nothing to be right or wrong about as between these two statements. Investigation under these conditions should extend to all cases to which the predicate can be applied. That actual and possible cases are both to be included would seem perfectly reasonable, not only under Carnap's conditions for the definition of the intension of a predicate, but under those of several other logicians. Thus C. I. Lewis writes:

"The comprehension of a term is the classification of all consistently thinkable things to which the term would correctly apply."[2]

One method of procedure would be to use modal expressions, though their ambiguity may always be raised as an objection. A much simpler method is to describe a fairy in a Latin formulation corresponding to the English: "An imaginary being of small and graceful form." Or one may take two pictures, one of a woman and the other of a fairy and compare the difference. All these three methods indicate that 1 and 2 above are different empirical hypotheses. The determination of intensions includes all logically possible cases, and this includes even those cases that are causally impossible.

The criticism of Quine is also vulnerable for a further reason.

These two definitions are customary in Latin-English diction-aries:

Monoceros, unicorn.

Nympha, fairy.

These entries would be considered most unusual:

Monoceros, fairy.

Nympha, unicorn.

The two Latin words, and the two Engish words, have the same extension, i.e. the null class. If Quine's standpoint is correct there is no empirically testable difference between these two groups of entries. The most that the non-intensionalist can say against this is that the first group of entries is acceptable and the second unacceptable on the authority of the tradition of lexi-cographers.

The empirical procedure for determining intensions and test-ing hypotheses concerning intensions has never been laid down at any great length.[3] However, as has been already indicated, such a procedure is possible, the general concept of the intension of any predicate in English or any other natural language having an empirically testable sense for any person under any given conditions. The intension of a predicate 'P' for a speaker S is the general condition which an object X must fulfill so that S shall be willing to ascribe the predicate 'P' to X. When it is said that S can communicate his ideas by means of a natural language L, the presupposition is that S has the interconnected faculties and the dispositions for communicating his thoughts. When it is said that a predicate 'P' in a natural language L has the property R as its intension for S, the presupposition is that among the faculties and dispositions of S which constitute the natural lan-guage L there is the predisposition to ascribe the predicate 'P' to any object X if and only if it has the property R. This principle is capable of further elaboration, so that two intensions, R_1 and R_2, can be included. The following statement will then be valid:

S has the faculties and dispositions of ascribing affirmatively the predicate 'P' to an object X if and only if X has R_1, and the faculties and dispositions of denying 'P' for X if and only if X has R_2. If for any reason whatsoever X has neither R_1 nor R_2, S cannot possibly give either a negative or an affirmative response. The zone of vagueness is then constituted as the property of having neither R_1 nor R_2.

There may be said to be two methods of categorising dispositional concepts. The first is an application of the fundamental tenets of behaviorism. Let S have a disposition D to react to any condition C by a response R. By this method the condition C will be produced, and then it can be determined whether R occurs or not. The second method, that of structural analysis, entails investigating the state of S at a given time t, so that it is possible to determine the responses which S would make under any given environmental circumstances. The application of the laws of other disciplines, e.g. psychology and physiology, would obviously be helpful at this stage. The distinction which Horzelski[4] makes between semantic and hedonic nuclei may well influence the trend of thinking on dispositional concepts. Once the state of S has been established, it should be possible to predict whether S would make the response R under the condition C. If S makes the response R, he has the disposition D; if R is not present, neither is D.

No one has drawn the distinction between 'analytic' (L- true) and 'synthetic' (factual) more clearly than Carnap.[5] Quine and White,[6] however, have further argued that there is no fundamental distinction between analytic and synthetic truths, regarding the differentiation as an aberration of modern empiricism, and that the most that can be said is that, if there is any distinction at all, it is one of degree and not of kind. These protests seem to present no really fundamental nullification of Carnap's original position on analytic.

Any intelligent discussion of analytic must, I assume, proceed relative to a language. The question under debate, then, is not so much that of 'analytic' as of 'analytic in L.' I take it that a sentence is analytic in L for a speaker S at any time t if its intension in L for S at t comprehends all possible cases. This definition covers not only the logical part of L but also its inconsistent areas, described in some detail by Tarski.[7]

Furthermore, there is a strong argument that ostensive definitions give rise to analytic statements, but one would hesitate to say that these are no different from synthetic statements. For example, a metre is defined as the length of the standard metre in Paris. In virtue of this definition, the sentence:

"The standard metre is one metre long."

can only mean:

"The standard metre has the length which is possessed by the standard metre."

i.e.:

"The standard metre has the length it has."

These statements arising from the original ostensive definition are analytic in virtue of their relation to the definition. Nobody will seriously suggest that they are synthetic.

Pap[8] takes virtually the same view. He regards an existential statement as a condensed version of a logical sum of elementary statements. Symbolically, this means that '(Ex) F(x)' is short for 'F(a) or F(b) . . . or F(n)' where a, b, . . . n are objects that may have the property F. Each of the logical alternatives is a merely probable statement, since there are empirical data which could falsify it. If, on the other hand, at least one of the alternatives should turn out to have the character of an ostensive definition, the existential statement would not be a dubitable empirical hypothesis, but would be analytic in the sense of being true by ostensive definition. Take the sentence:

"There exists at least one rod which has exactly the length of one metre."

This sentence is equivalent to the sum:

"Either a is one metre long or b has that property . . .
or n has that property."

where the series a . . . n includes all the rods in the universe.
With respect to n—one meter rods in the universe, it is a question of fact whether their length is or is not exactly one metre.
But if the expression "one metre" is to have any meaning at all,
one rod in the universe must have the predicated property by
ostensive definition, i.e. the standard metre in Paris. Hence the
existential statement given above must be analytic, and cannot
possibly be synthetic, as it is both significant and true by ostensive definition.

The further suggestion of Quine is that, though there is no
significant difference between the analytic and the synthetic,
"there is a gulf between meaning and naming." As it stands, this
would seem to represent an inconsistency. The correct interpretation may be that, since names can be eliminated in favor of the
reference of bound variables, there is strictly no gulf between
naming and meaning, or for that matter, between naming and
anything else. All that is left after names have been eliminated
is reference with its "studied ambiguity," and meaning. This
interpretation is further backed by Quine's own words that,
when the cleavage between meaning and reference is properly
heeded, "the problems . . . become separated into two prov-
inces . . . fundamentally distinct . . ." The gulf, then, would
appear to be between meaning and reference.

If Quine's words are interpreted literally, the symbolic repre-
sentation is this:

$$M/N \cdot \sim (A/S)$$

where:

$$
\begin{aligned}
M &= \text{Meaning} \\
N &= \text{Naming} \\
/ &= \text{The gulf between the two} \\
A &= \text{Analytic} \\
S &= \text{Synthetic}
\end{aligned}
$$

The universe of discourse is regarded as a field of force, bounded by experience of the external world, and constituted of two components:

a. The empirical force extending into the field from the external word, and being stronger near the periphery.
b. The formal or logical force, extending outward from its strongest point, the center, and having simplicity and symmetry of laws as its principle.

These are, I take it, the elements of the unified field theory which seems in most respects to be virtually the same as the so-called theory of signification. Statements are distributed in this field. Though "it is misleading to speak of the empirical content" of any isolated statement, it is even more misleading when the statement "is at all remote from the experimental periphery of the field." This is the case because such statements are determined primarily by consideration of their meaning. Since a gulf exists between the meaning of statements and their referential significance manifesting what is designated, the statements "having meaning" may be said to be intelligible without considering the entities referred to. As Quine observes in the case of the statement:

"The Evening Star is the Morning Star,"

the Babylonian Astronomer "could have dispensed with his observations, and contented himself with reflecting on the meanings of his words." If such a consideration were to reveal a synonymy, the proposition could have been asserted *a priori*, but in fact the key terms in this statement also function as names. They not only possess meaning, but they refer to any object, (or purport to refer to it), and this is their existential reference. Their significance in this mode of signifying is the object referred to, for if there is no object, there can be no genuine name.

Working from Quine's premisses, it seems logically impossible to know whether there are any genuine names. To know that the term T is a name would be to know that what it names exists, and not merely to believe or posit it. Posits and beliefs can be mistaken to the extent that there are not sufficient for the occurrence of a genuine name which must have an existing object as its referent or designatum, and this would be a contradiction in terms, considered in Quine's frame of reference. He must deny that genuine names are known to occur, or else he is bound to assert that certain entities are known absolutely to exist, a conclusion which would necessarily conflict with his general linguistic relativism. This he admits to a point when he says that "perhaps we can reach no absolute decision as to which words have designata." But surely we cannot possibly reach any absolute decision when he views any significant decision as being possible only within the inner unified field of conceptualization of meaning, itself relative and determined by what he refers to as "our culture." I feel that the only possible conclusion from Quine's hypotheses is that none of our terms is a genuine name, at least in the strict sense of an expression performing the operation of designation.

Arguing from this position, Aldrich[9] attempted to show that, though Quine intended to say:

$$M/N \cdot \sim (A/S),$$

he implicitly intended:

$$\sim (A/S) \supset \sim (M/N)$$

or

$$M/N \cdot \supset \cdot A/S.$$

In other words, since Quine abandoned the dichotomy between synthetic and analytic, he is in effect working with the notion of continuity and degrees as applied to both meaning and reference. Though I find Aldrich's discussion periphrastic and rambling in places, I believe his contention, that one cannot abandon A/S without abandoning M/N, to be valid and that Quine implicitly accepted the formula of the older empirical position:

$$(M/N) \cdot \equiv \cdot (A/S).$$

I am not wholly in favor of Aldrich's explanation of Quine's preference of M/N over (A/S) as the result of his incipient, fundamentally Kantian, metaphysical and epistemological dualism. I find no direct relationship between Quine's position and that of metaphysical dualism. Is this not possibly reading into Quine's work something that was never intended?

A further problem arises from expressions which possess likeness of meaning. An arresting conclusion made by Goodman[10] is the falsity of the sentence:

"There are some typographically different expressions in English and other natural (and symbolic) languages which are synonymous."

In support of this contention, two arguments are proposed, one based on Goodman's plea for the adoption of a certain new criterion for synonymy, the other upon a semantical principle which is a natural requirement that is normally made upon any satisfactory criterion of synonymy, but which leads, as he shows, to the negation of the quoted sentence. If Goodman's second argument is correct, the sentence would have to be repudiated nonarbitrarily, so that its denial by his proposed criterion would definitely be in his favor.

The principle of semantics basic to the second argument is this.[11] Let 'c' and 'd' be any two synonymous expressions and let '. . . d . . .' be formed from '. . . c . . .' by substituting 'd' for some occurrence of 'c.' If '. . . c . . .' is a nonintensional context, then it has the same truth-value as '. . . d . . .'. If this be granted, then Goodman only has to establish two further points:

1. The predicate 'is a c- description' is nonintensional, and is not a context in which such words as 'necessary,' 'possible' or 'thought of' occur.

2. For any two expressions 'c' and 'd' which differ typographically, there is an inscription D such that 'D is a c- description' changes its truth-value when 'd' is substituted for 'c'.

It follows that the quoted sentence must be false.

It will be seen immediately that the principle which has been outlined is not among the natural demands made upon any criterion of synonymy. It forces the conclusion that the words 'ruler' and 'governor' are not synonymous simply because they cannot be interreplaced in the context:

'Ruler' contains the letters R-u-l-e-r, in that order.

The principal strength of Goodman's argument lies in the appearance 'c' and 'd' have of functioning as independent word units in 'is a c- description' and 'is a d- description,' unlike expressions which function only as parts of such independent units, e.g. the word 'governor' in the expression 'governor-general.' Then bearing in mind the notion of the independent word unit, we may rephrase Goodman's principle thus. Let 'c' and 'd' be formed from '. . . c . . .' by substituting 'd' for some occurrence of 'c' functioning as an independent word unit. If '. . . c . . .' is a nonintensional context, then it has the same truth value as '. . . d . . .'. (Incidentally, Goodman hyphenates his predicate not to indicate that 'c' and 'd' are parts of it but simply as a visual reminder that 'description of' is not a relation in the sense in which Russell and Whitehead use it in the *Principia Mathematica*. Thus the more natural form of the predicate is 'is a description of c's'.)

Vital to Goodman's argument, then, is the naturalness of the principle just outlined and the appearance that 'c' does occur in 'is a c- description' as an independent word unit. He is only concerned with explaining his predicate as applied to inscriptions of the form '. . . that is not——,' and so we must know under what circumstances this form is a description of c's. Normally '. . . that is not ——' is a description of c's if it selected some c's and only c's from the universe. Thus 'a pungent odor that is not an acrid odor' is description of pungent odors but not of acrid ones. But what of phrases such as 'hobgoblin that is not a fairy'? Here the requirement may reasonably be relaxed; '. . . that is not ——' is a description of c's if and only if it purports to be true of c's, even though there may be none. One method of avoiding the difficulty would be to rule out descriptions the extension of which is null, but these are precisely the D's that are needed to show that for any two expressions 'c' and 'd' differing typographically, there is an inscription D such that 'D is a c-description' changes its truth-value when 'd' is substituted for 'c'.

This may be established by maintaining that for any two expressions 'c' and 'd', the appropriate D is 'c that is not d'—as Goodman suggests. The only exception that I take to this is that there would seem to be a natural sense in which 'hobgoblin that· is not a fairy' *purports* to be true of hobgoblins only. To take an even clearer case, there is a sense in which 'triangle that is not trilateral' *purports* to be about triangles, though not about trilateral figures. But having made this point acceptable we have cast doubt on the predicate's 'is a c- description' being nonintensional, since the notion of purport involves tacit references to the intentions of speakers or the interpretations of listeners. Hence any context using the notion would seem to be not, at least *prima facie*, nonintensional.

I believe that this potential objection to Goodman's predicate may be answered by interpreting the context of the predicate as being elliptical for one referring to the objective circumstances under which expressions do purport. For example, the stipulation that X must occur in English in the position which pronouns may occupy is a specification of the conditions under which X purports to name one and only one object, as Quine[12] has indicated. The expansion of Goodman's context will be virtually the same, though more elaborate. It must answer the question of under what conditions '. . . that is not ——' purports to be true only of c's, and if valid conditions can be found, Goodman's contention will hold good.

I believe these conditions are discoverable, though slight rephrasings of Goodman's argument seem inevitable. This is a true sentence:

'Mother that is not a female parent' purports to be true only of mothers.

How many different expressions may be substituted for the occurrences of 'mother' and 'female parent' in this sentence, and still yield only true variants of the sentence, provided that they are acceptable grammatically? So long as the substituted expressions are meaningful, and the same typographically identical expression is substituted for both occurrences of 'mother,' the resulting variant of Goodman's original conclusion, that there are some typographically different expressions in English and other natural languages which are synonymous, is undeniably true. Incidentally, Goodman decides that 'c that is not c' is not within the range of significance of 'is a c- description.' This seems to be in the nature of a borderline case, and here, surely, the meaning of the predicate does not sanction one interpretation or the other, though a method of dealing with this and similar situations would be to disallow substitutions that resulted in the form 'c that is not c.'

It is possible to go one stage further and maintain that the substituted expressions need not even be meaningful.[13] This sentence is also true:

'Bang that is not bong' purports to be true only of bangs.

The typographical requirement alone is necessary, and so Goodman's context may be rephrased in objective terms:

" '. . . that is not ——' is a c- description"

is elliptical for

" '. . . that is not ——' has 'c' in the position . . ."

where the 'c' used by the original predicate is mentioned in the expansion. The meaning of D being a c- description is that the expression 'c' occurs in a certain position within D, and D is of the form '. . . that is not ——.' Goodman's argument would seem to be valid, but rests on the intuitive understanding of his predicate 'is a c- description.'

Goodman has also suggested that a difference in meaning between two predicates is always accompanied by a difference in their primary or secondary extensions, where a secondary extension of a word is the extension of a compound having that word as a component. He argues that for every pair of predicates there is a corresponding pair of compounds, formed by identical additions (e.g. "——description") to the two predicates, which do not apply to the same things. Thus if identity of primary and secondary extension is adopted as a criterion of synonymy, two different predicates can never have the same meaning, even if they exhibit some degree of likeness of meaning.

This standpoint has been attacked by Rudner[14] who maintains an alternative view. If one takes the standpoint of a vigorous nominalism, that not words or statements, but only inscriptions or parts of inscriptions are meaningful, one could maintain that no repetitive inscription is analytic, for no two of its constituent parts have the same primary or secondary extensions.

As it stands, this argument seems invalid. First, it is notoriously difficult to decide what should be taken as appropriate compounds to show that two predicate-inscriptions, say I_1 and I_2 differ in secondary extension. If I_1 and I_2 are to be constituent parts of the compounds they must exist as so many marks within these compounds. But each can exist as part of only one compound, since the same inscription cannot occur at different places or at different times. Different temporal parts of the total history of a mark may be virtually different words. Thus a sign saying "No Parking Here" may be moved about, and the temporal connotation of "Here" will vary according to the different locations in which the sign is placed. But if I_1 or I_2 does not happen to occur compounded it will not have a secondary extension. In general, then, it seems to me that if the compounds corresponding to two predicate-inscriptions can be formed by additions to the predicate-inscriptions themselves, then most predicate-inscriptions, being uncompounded, will not possess secondary extension. Among these predicate-inscriptions, those with identical primary extensions will be synonymous, since they will also have the same secondary extension by virtue of having none.

A further solution is provided by Robbins.[15] Preferring the term event to inscription, he urges that where two sign-events would ordinarily be regarded as instances of the same sign-design, they should be called "replicas" of one another. Thus any "unicorn"—event is a replica of itself and of every other "unicorn"-event. The relation of "being a replica of" is reflexive, symmetric and transitive. Rudner may prefer to construe this sentence:

$$\text{"}I_1 \text{ occurs in the compound } C_1\text{"}$$

as expressing elliptically that a replica of I_1 is part of a replica of C_1. But every two predicate-events which are replicas of each other occur in exactly the same compounds. Inevitably, then, if two such predicate-events have the same primary extension, they will also have the same secondary extensions.

It is impossible to treat the question of meaning adequately without reference to the so-called paradox of analysis. Langford[16] states it thus:

"If the verbal expression representing the analysandum has the same meaning as the verbal expression representing the analysans, the analysis states a bare identity and is trivial; but if the two verbal expressions do not have the same meaning, the analysis is incorrect."

The distinction may be made in two sentences:

a. 'The concept Wife is identical with the concept Married Woman.'
b. 'The concept Wife is identical with the concept Wife.'

The first sentence states the result of an analysis of the analysandum, the concept Wife, and conveys logical, though not factual information. The second sentence conveys virtually no logical information and is tautologous of its nature. Moore[17] presumes that if the first sentence is true, the second would appear

to make the same statement. This follows, because, if two concepts are identical, a reference to one means the same as a reference to the other, and thus one expression can be replaced by
the other. This reasoning is fallacious because, as Moore himself
admits, it is patently obvious that these two statements are not
the same. The discussion that ensued in the pages of "Mind"
between 1944 and 1945 was largely nullified by the fact that
none of the controversialists stated any criteria for the meaning
of "meaning." Obviously it is ridiculous to say that a sentence is
meaningless (as was said of sentence b) before we know what
meaning is.

I believe that the first step in attempting to solve the paradox
is to state the exact difference in meaning between the two sentences a and b and then to discover how this difference is
compatible with the analysis of meaning which I have outlined
early in this paper. Certainly the two sentences are L- equivalent
and L- true to each other, and thus express the same proposition.
The difference lies elsewhere. It seems to me to be one of intensional structure, for the analysans is more articulate than the
analysandum and is a grammatical function manifesting more
than one idea. The two expressions, then, are not synonymous
but only "cognitively equivalent," to use Langford's expression.
The concept of L- equivalence is applicable here, and that of intensional isomorphism for the synonymity which does not hold
for these expressions.

The method of meaning analysis for which I have argued is
based, with some slight variations, on that of Carnap and C. I.
Lewis. Thus Lewis[18] writes:

"All terms have meaning in the sense or mode of denotation or extension; and all have meaning in the mode of connotation or intension. The denotation of a term is the class
of all actual or existent things to which that term correctly
applies. . . . The comprehension of a term is the classification of all consistently thinkable things to which the term

could correctly apply. . . . The connotation or intension of a term is delimited by any correct definition of it."

It is when Lewis follows Meinong in elaborating a concept of comprehension which presupposes the admission of nonactual, possible things, that I am inclined to differ. What Lewis writes is a perfectly valid development from the premisses of Meinong, but it is with these premisses that the difference commences. Meinong[19] differentiated between all things that are possible and all things that are impossible. Possible things can be further subdivided into actual possible things (e.g. man), and nonactual possible things (e.g. unicorn). Russell rejected Meinong's position because the impossible objects violate the principle of contradiction, and this objection has since been reinforced by Ryle with additional argumentation. Russell was surely right, for the ordinary language will not consistently bear the conception of impossible things or even of nonactual possible things. It is obviously a violation of natural language to say that a round square is both round and nonround because it is square. Perhaps one day a philosopher will construct a language system to accommodate these cases, but to my knowledge none exists at present.

I take it that there is virtually no difference between the purposes of the concepts of comprehension and intension. Therefore, instead of dividing objects into the three groups impossible, actual possible and nonactual possible, I differentiate between the corresponding expressions and their intensions. The three sentences that follow are in Meinong's terminology:

1. 'Round squares are impossible objects.'
2. 'Fairies are nonactual possible objects.'
3. 'Men are actual possible objects.'

These may be thus translated, with reference to their predicators:

1. 'The predicator 'round square' is L- empty.'

2. 'The predicator 'fairy' is empty but not L- empty.'
3. 'The predicator 'man' is not empty.'

Applying these terms to the corresponding intensions, the sentences become:

1. 'The property Round Square is L- empty.'
2. 'The property Fairy is empty but not L- empty.'
3. 'The property Man is not empty.'

Analogous distinctions can be made for individual expressions, applying the distinctions to intensions, instead of to objects as would be done by Meinong and Lewis. As an example I shall take a description. Here are three formulations referring to objects and using Meinong's method and order:

1. 'Plato's garden is an actual object' (presuming that the histories of Plato are correct).
2. 'Plato's phoenix is a nonactual possible object.'
3. 'Plato's round square is an impossible object.'

These become when translated:

1. 'The description 'Plato's garden' is not empty.'
2. 'The description 'Plato's phoenix' is empty but not L-empty (i.e. it has zero denotation but not zero comprehension).'
3. 'The description 'Plato's round square' is L- empty (i.e. it has zero denotation and zero comprehension).'

Corresponding statements can be made of individual concepts:

1. 'The individual concept Plato's garden is not empty.'
2. 'The individual concept Plato's phoenix is empty but not L-empty.'
3. 'The individual concept Plato's Round Square is L-empty.'

The threefold distinction of Meinong is also vulnerable from the standpoint of modal logic. The logical modalities, I submit, cannot be applied to extensions and must be applied to intensions. One may speak of an L- false or impossible proposition, but not of an L- false or impossible truth-value. One may speak of an L- empty property or individual concept, but not of an L- empty class or individual object. Objects are extensions, not intensions; individuals are involved in questions of application, not in questions of meaning. Hence any attempt to define meaning in natural languages must commence with the scientific analysis of intension, a procedure which is now achieving the same respectable status as the analysis of the pragmatical concepts of the theory of extension.

NOTES

1. Quine, W. V.: "Two Dogmas of Empiricism" in "Philosophical Review," 60: 20–43 (1951). Reprinted in "From a Logical Point of View: Nine Logical-Philosophical Essays" (1953). See especially p. 63.
2. Lewis, C. I.: "The Modes of Meaning" in *Philosophy and Phenomenological Research*, 4:236–250 (1944).
3. For pioneer work in this almost unexplored field see:
   Carnap, R.: "Meaning and Synonymy in Natural Languages," in *Philosophical Studies*, Vol. VI, No. 3, Apr. 1955.
   Naess, A.: "Interpretation and Preciseness: A Contribution to the Theory of Communication." (Skrifter Norske Vid. Akademi, Oslo, II, Hist—Filos. Klasse, 1953, No. 1.)
4. Horzelski, J.: "Remarks on The Psychology of Language," in *Philosophy*, Vol. XXX, No. 112, Jan. 1955.
5. Vide:
   Carnap, R.: "Meaning and Necessity," University of Chicago Press, 1947 and "The Logical Foundations of Probability," University of Chicago Press, 1950, Ch. III.
6. Vide:
   Quine, W. V.: "Two Dogmas of Empiricism," in *Philosophical Review*, 60:20–43 (1951).
   White, M. G.: "The Analytic and the Synthetic: An Untenable Dualism," in "John Dewey: Philosopher of Science and Freedom," ed. by S. Hook, Dial Press, 1950, pp. 316–330.
   An interesting discussion of these papers is provided in:
   Mates, B.: "Analytic Sentences," in *Philosophical Review*, 60: 525–534 (1951).
   Martin, R. M.: "On Analytic," *Philosophical Studies*, Vol. III, No. 3, April 1952.

7. Tarski, A.: "Der Wahrheitsbegriff in den formalisierten Sprach-
en," in *Studia Philosophica*, 1:261–405 (1936), esp. pp. 267–
279.
8. Pap, A.: "Indubitable Existential Statements" in *Mind,* Vol. LV
(1946) pp. 234–246.
Also relevant is the series of articles "Analytic-Synthetic" by
Friedrich Waismann appearing in various editions of *Analysis*
between 1949 and 1952.
9. Aldrich, V. C.: "Mr. Quine on Meaning, Naming and Purporting
to Name," in *Philosophical Studies*, Vol. VI, No. 2, Feb.
1955.
10. Goodman, N.: "On Likeness of Meaning" in *Analysis*, 10 (No.
1):1–7 (Oct. 1949).
11. In the discussion that follows 'c' and 'd' represent the names of
those expressions which c and d represent.
12. Quine, W. V.: "Methods of Logic." New York: Holt, (1951) p.
205.
13. This further idea was suggested by Robert Price's article "A Note
on Likeness of Meaning," in *Analysis*, Vol. 11, pp. 18–19.
14. Rudner, R.: "A Note on Likeness of Meaning," in *Analysis*,
Vol. 10, pp. 115–118, (1949–1950).
15. Robbins, B. L.: "On Synonymy of Word Events," in *Analysis*,
Vol. 12, p. 100 (1952).
16. Langford, C. H.: "The Notion of Analysis in Moore's Philosophy"
in "The Philosophy of G. E. Moore," ed. P. Schilpp (1942), p.
323.
17. Op. cit. pp. 660–667.
18. Lewis, C. I.: "The Modes of Meaning," in *Philosophy and
Phenomenological Research*, IV (1943–44), pp. 236–250.
19. Meinong, A. von: "Untersuchungen zur Gegenstandstheorie und
Psychologie," Leipzig, 1904.

The Completeness of the
Sentential Calculus

HISTORICALLY, the fundamentals of the sentential calculus were laid down by Peirce and Schroder and were deduced from Boole's system of the two-valued algebra. The difficulty about the older method of developing the calculus lay chiefly in its circularity as a deductive system. The logic of propositions had to be given antecedently before the deduction was possible, and the principles deduced were those of the logic of propositions. Obviously this was unsatisfactory, even though the laws of logic were not necessarily invalidated by the fact that they could not be deduced unless they were first taken for granted as principles of their own deduction.

In order to avoid this circularity, contemporary logicians have, for the most part, abandoned this method, and have resorted to the logistic method of *Principia Mathematica*. Here the principles of logic are not antecedently presumed as rules of demonstration. Instead of this procedure, the rules in accordance with which proofs are given are rules of more or less mechanical operations upon the symbols, such as rules allowing certain substitutions to be made in the postulates or in theorems that have already been proved.

Logical truth, according to the more recent method, is attained by developing the calculus of sentences in the first instance. This entails primarily the tabulation of rules which can be stated for all sentences, without reference to their analysis into terms and relations of terms. From the calculus of sentences we derive the calculus of sentential functions, and from this we derive the calculus of classes and the calculus of relations. Even though there is necessarily some difference in the content of particular branches contingent upon this logistic development in contradistinction to the older non-logistic procedure, the really important distinction between them is that of method, and, generally speaking, the contents are the same.

In spite of its evident superiority, the discussion of the logistic method is still fraught with unsolved problems. For instance, the question whether the sentential calculus completely formalizes all logical features of the part of logic covered by it, has never been fully answered to anything like general satisfaction. Furthermore, there has generally been an unconscious fusion of syntactical and semantical terms in the metalanguage commonly used by logicians. The word "completeness" has been variously interpreted. Gödel, in discussing his theorem concerning the completeness of the so-called lower functional calculus, similar to the functional calculus but containing predicate variables, formulates it in two ways:

1. "Every formula (i.e. sentential function of the calculus in question) which is universally valid is provable."
2. "Every formula is either refutable or satisfiable."

I distinguish two types of terminology in these formulations. The terms "provable" and "refutable" are obviously syntactical, having been defined on the basis of the rules of the lower functional calculus, explicitly stated in the form of primitive sentences and rules of inference. The terms "universally valid" (*allgemeingultig*) and "satisfiable" (*erfullbar*) are quite clearly semantical, being explained thus. A formula (a sentential function of the calculus in question) is universally valid if it is true for all values of the free variables; it is satisfiable if there are values of the free variables for which it is true. Godel's theorem combines syntactical and semantical concepts in a way which he himself, perhaps, did not fully realise. If it were more exactly formulated, it would state a relation between a syntactical and a corresponding semantical system.

The first attempt to demonstrate conclusively the completeness of the sentential calculus was made by Post in 1921,[1] and since then more details have been filled into substantially the same proof by Hilbert, Ackermann and Bernays.[2] During the same period some radically different proofs have also appeared.[3] The failure to differentiate between syntactical and semantical concepts in almost all these proofs has been largely responsible for so much inexact delineation of the problems involved.

Some authors have tackled the question, given attention to the investigation of the issues, and abandoned the whole sentential calculus as a science of logical inference. Nordenson[4] provides a not too uncommon attitude. He argues that as the content of any logical proposition consists of statements concerning the truth possibilities of its argument propositions, and these contents are identical, the proofs of completeness and rules of inference are superfluous. In spite of the tautological nature of logical propositions, it may seem possible on occasions to read (*auszulesen*) the various formulae in the sentential calculus as so many different logical propositions, but this is only because the logical constants are expressed by words, and this does not exactly cover the contents of the constants as defined by the truth-tables. If they are read correctly, the contents of all the formulae are identical, and it is consequently impossible to base any logical argumentation on them. Finally he urges that the sentential calculus is useless for drawing conclusions. The best use that it can serve is to register results which could quite easily have been obtained by means of classical logic independently of any formula.

This view has been reiterated periodically, and seems to me to be based largely on the refusal to allow a difference between the formal and material exposition of logic, and between object-language and syntax-language. One would have thought that

Wittgenstein had explained and justified the tautological nature of logical propositions to most people's satisfaction, but there are logicians who remained unconvinced, without being able to prove Wittgenstein wrong. The constant discussions on the disparity of the defined logical constants and the corresponding words in natural languages are surely ample manifestation of this. One of the most important functions of formulae is that they calculate results in highly complicated cases where classical methods, because of their comparative lack of development in the field of semiotics, cannot possibly compete. At some time in the future a philosopher may develop the classical procedures to cover complex semiotical cases, but to my knowledge the requisite logical machinery is not in existence at present.

It is essential to differentiate between the various methods of constructing the sentential calculus, and particularly between the procedure applying primitive sentences and rules of inference, and that applying truth-tables. These two methods are sometimes regarded as being, for all intents and purposes, equivalent ways of representing the ordinary sentential calculus, though in fact they are fundamentally different. The method of primitive sentences and rules of inference is formal, and belongs to the sphere of syntax. The method of truth-tables states truth-conditions for the sentences and gives an interpretation. It is therefore part of semantics. I omit for the present purpose the lesser developed formal method of value-tables, sometimes known as matrices, which is analogous to that of truth-tables, but does not involve the concept of truth. I believe that a system which applies truth-tables should not be classed as a sentential calculus at all. The term "sentential logic" appears more applicable.[5] The construction of the sentential calculus, then, should be limited to primitive sentences and rules of inference.

The concern of the constructors of the sentential calculus has been far more restricted than is sometimes realized. In the first place, they are interested only with sentences whose meaning can be given by entailment rules and secondly only a relatively small subclass of extremely general entailment rules is ever used, wittingly or unwittingly, in sentential calculus construction. This consideration helps to explain the quite limited area covered by the five primitive propositions put forward by Whitehead and Russell in *Principia Mathematica* from which the remaining laws of the system were to be deduced. The five primitive propositions and the laws deducible from them are reproduced in the table below:

Primitive Propositions	Laws
$p \vee p \supset p$	Tautology
$q \supset p \vee q$	Addition
$p \vee q \supset q \vee p$	Permutation
$(q \supset r) \supset (p \vee q \supset p \vee r)$	Summation
$q \vee (q \vee r) \supset q \vee (p \vee r)$	Association

There are three considerations affecting the selection of a set of initial laws. First, the undefined constants of the system should be consistent, so as not to include any formula of the form "p· ⌐ p". Secondly, any formula which can be shown to be analytic should be derivable, by using the higher-order principles of inference, from these five postulates. Thirdly, the number of primitive propositions and the number of undefined constants should be the minimum which is consistent with the satisfaction of the essential requirement of adequacy. This third requirement is not met by the set provided by Whitehead and Russell, since the fifth proposition is superfluous.

From the logician's point of view, the ideal type of sentence is one which, if delivered at any time, at any place, by any speaker results in a true statement, then its delivery at any other time, at any other place, by any other speaker results in a true statement. There would appear to be only a small number of types of sentences which can realize this ideal, positively and negatively existential sentences being principal examples. In existential sentences "(ᴲx)" is either timeless or omnitemporal and should not be temporally ambiguous. Furthermore, such sentences need contain no expression which functions as a logical subject, and they are entirely free from referring elements.

The majority of statement-making sentences that are in use, or could be used in everyday speech, have no place in the framing of any existing logical calculus. The attempt of some philosophers to utilize the so-called logically proper name, envisaged as a type of referring expression free from the unideal characteristics of all other referring expressions, seems quite purposeless as it takes for granted the existence of such names in the first place. If there really were a class of expressions, the meaning of which was identical with a single object, the problem under discussion would not exist. A sentence of the form "fx," where the predicate replacing "f" was omnitemporal and the individual expression replacing "x" was an expression of this class, would have all the timeless, placeless and impersonal qualities of the logical ideal. The structure of quantificational logic has always required that there should be individual referring expressions which could exist as values of the individual variables. In other words, logicians have tended to pre-suppose the existence of simple predicative sentences of the "fx" variety. This presupposition was supported by the belief in logically proper names and helped in disseminating the idea that these sentences were of the logically ideal type. The general confusion between a sentence and a statement assisted in clouding the general issue, so that far stronger claims were made for the adequacy of general symbolic procedures than were actually justifiable.

A further confusion is made on occasions over the distinction between the sentential calculus and calculi containing the sentential calculus. Calculi are sometimes constructed by logicians which do not contain the sentential calculus but represent the sentential calculus itself in a pure form, containing propositional variables as the only ultimate components. In this type of calculus every sentence is open, where otherwise one would have expected closed sentences, and all of them are either provable (C-true) or C- comprehensive, being derivable from the calculus (C- implicate of it). When discussing the interpretation of sentences, this is a distinct disadvantage. The usual interpretation is L- true, and thus all sentences in the pure form of the sentential calculus become L- determinate. There are no factual sentences in this case. As the normal truth-tables only apply to closed sentences they cannot be used here. In most of the research connected with symbolic logic, one is dealing not so much with pure forms of the sentential calculus as with calculi containing the sentential calculus. It is therefore important to bear in mind the ways in which the features of the more comprehensive calculus influence the properties of the sentential calculus as such.

As a tentative step towards the solution of these problems in the general area of formal system construction, I distinguish between four uses of the word "completeness":

1. Every sentence in a given sentential calculus is either provable or refutable, i.e., its negation is provable.
2. Every sentence in a given sentential calculus with propositional variables as the only ultimate components is either provable or refutable.
3. Every sentence in a given sentential calculus which is L-true by the ordinary truth-tables is provable.
4. If a form SC of a given sentential calculus, constructed with propositional variables as the only atomic sentences, has a new calculus SC^1 constructed out of it by declaring any sentence S of SC as an additional primitive sentence, then S is either already provable in SC or not.

It will be noted that, though these uses vary, they all contain the adjective "provable." An initial step in the formulation of a concise definition of the *idea* of completeness in formal systems is to replace the customary term "completeness" by two variations of what I shall term substantively as "C-truth." Uses 1 to 3 are all applicable to sentences in one given sentential calculus and are the more traditional conceptions of completeness. For these cases, I suggest the term "General C-truth." Case 4 applies to two given sentential calculi related to one another and is a much more recent and circumscribed conception. For this case the term "Strict C-truth" seems applicable. As I indicated earlier, it seems rather doubtful whether case 3 could properly be categorized under the title of sentential calculus at all, but I include it as a traditional usage.

An essential property which sentences must possess for inclusion in a given sentential calculus is logical form. This requirement needs emphasis, particularly as Russell and other authors speak as if logical form were a property of propositions rather than sentences. The grammatical form of a sentence is a discernible structural property of that sentence. The logical form of a sentence is the grammatical form that the sentence would have in an ideal language, i.e., ideal for indicating the logical relations that sentences have to one another. It does not necessarily follow that in an ideal language one can immediately tell the logical relation of a number of sentences, but the structure of the sentences would enable the procedure sometimes called "derivation" to prevent the giving of a wrong answer to the question: "What is the logical relation of sentence A to sentence B and sentence C?"

My suggestion that the logical form of a sentence is the grammatical form that the sentence ought to have may perhaps indicate why so many philosophers have attributed logical form to propositions rather than sentences. The grammatical form is given and observable, the logical form is often hidden by the grammatical form. Thus some other object which has this form is produced, and if the proposition is not brought in here, recourse is had to the distinction between a language and some other non-linguistic entity which language expresses. Although sentences do have logical relations to one another, their grammatical structure does not always indicate clearly what the logical relations are. One may be inclined to feel that these two sentences are contradictories:

1. The present king of France is bald.
2. The present king of France is not bald.

Russell argued that these are not contradictories; Frege argued that they are. An ideal language would indicate perfectly clearly, at least by translation, the exact logical relation between these two sentences, and the grammatical structure of the sentence would be a reliable indicator of its logical properties.

I have suggested that the term "completeness" is ambiguous, and is best replaced by other terminology, e.g. General C-Truth and Strict C-Truth. A much firmer clarification between syntactical and semantical concepts involved and a solution of the outstanding problems in logical form are also essential before sharper definitions of the sentential calculus and the *idea* of its completeness can be constructed. The result may very possibly mean not only the abandonment of the concept of completeness in its present form, but also the development of a hybrid-type calculus embodying the significant advances that have been made recently in distinguishing syntax and semantics.

NOTES

1. Post, E. L.: "Introduction to a General Theory of Elementary Propositions," in *American Journal of Mathematics,* Vol. 43 (1921), pp. 167–173.
2. Hilbert and Ackermann: *"Grundzuge der Theoretischen Logik,"* Berlin, 1928, pp. 9–29.
   Hilbert and Bernays: *"Grundlagen der Mathematik,"* Vol. I, Berlin, 1934, pp. 49–67.
3. For example:
   (1) Lukasiewicz: *"Ein Vollständigkeitsbeweis des Sweiwertigen Aussagenkalküls,"* in *"Comptes Rendus des Séances de la Société des Sciences et des Lettres de Varsovie,"* Classe III, Vol. 24, 1931, pp. 153–183.
   (2) Kalmar: *"Ueber die Axiomatisierbarkeit des Aussagenkalküls,"* in *"Acta Litterarum ac Scientiarum Regiae Universitatis Hungaricae Francisco—Josephinae,"* Sectio Scientarium Mathematicarum, Vol. 7, 1935, pp. 222–243.
   (3) Hermes and Scholz: *"Ein Neuer Vollständigkeitsbeweis fur das Reduzierte Fregesche Axiomensystem des Aussagenkalküls,"* Leipzig, 1937.
   (4) Quine, W. V.: "Completeness of the Propositional Calculus,"

in *Journal of Symbolic Logic*, Vol. 3, No. 1 March, 1938, pp. 37–40.

4. Nordenson, H.: *"Kritische Bemerkungen zu den Grundlagen der Logistik,"* in "Adolph Phalen in memoriam, Philosophical Essays," Uppsala and Stockholm, 1937, pp. 486–545.

5. Or "propositional logic," to use Carnap's term.

On Mathematical Definition

THE view that definitions are superfluous has been elaborated at some length in *Principia Mathematica*. Whitehead and Russell thus state their position:

"A definition is a declaration that a certain newly-introduced symbol or combination of symbols is to mean the same as a certain other combination of symbols of which the meaning is already known. . . . Theoretically it is unnecessary ever to give a definition: we might always use the *definiens* instead, and thus wholly dispense with the *definiendum*. . . .

"In spite of the fact that definitions are theoretically superfluous, it is nevertheless true that they often convey more important information than is contained in the propositions in which they are used. This arises from two causes. First, a definition usually implies that the *definiens* is worthy of careful consideration. Hence the collection of definitions embodies our choice of subjects and our judgment as to what is most important. Secondly, when what is defined is (as often occurs) something already familiar, such as cardinal or ordinal numbers, the definition contains an analysis of a common idea, and may therefore express a notable advance."[1]

While pointing out that all definitions are theoretically unnecessary, allowance was made for stipulative abbreviations. An example of such an abbreviation is manifested in 'i,' a short form of the older phrase, "The square root of minus one." Even these are not always strictly necessary, as the authors admit. One can always write '$\sqrt{-1}$' instead of the abbreviation, making the writing of the statement longer, but embodying the same ideas as before.

Nevertheless, the majority of definitions in mathematical systems are not stipulative abbreviations. In implying that the definiendum is an idea, the authors contradict their definition of "definition," according to which the definiendum is a symbol. Furthermore, in maintaining that the definiendum is often "something already familiar," they contradict their previous doctrine that the definiendum is by definition "newly-introduced." Surely a definition in mathematics is often a real definition in the sense of an analysis of an old idea. It is often not a declaration that a certain new symbol is to mean the same as a certain combination of old symbols, but rather that a certain old symbol does mean the same as a certain combination of old symbols. Their definition, that 'p implies q,' is equivalent to 'either p is false or q is true,' was intended as an analysis of the old idea of implication, and even though I consider that this analysis is not correct, it would seem to constitute a type of definition not external to the system.

When a logician sets about the task of definition he is attempting to analyse an idea in terms of a set of ideas. Tarski has thus described this process: . . . "to put correctly the question how a certain concept is to be defined, one must first give a list of the terms by means of which one intends to construct the desired definition."[2] The aim in this type of logical definition is to present a certain form as a complex of other forms, and to include these other forms in a set of primitive ideas. As Tarski[3] further shows, there are two parallel processes working simultaneously, that of proving as many theorems as possible from as few axioms as possible, and that of defining as many concepts as possible from as few primitive concepts as possible.

An idea is indefinable relative to a given set of primitive ideas if it cannot be analysed into any function of that set. The indefinability should not detract from the value of definitions of ideas in general. It is only relative inasmuch as an idea which is indefinable relative to one set of principles may be definable relative to another. Furthermore, it is not an indefinability of words but of ideas. A word, *qua se,* is never incapable of definition.

There is a paradox which exists in the framing of definitions in symbolic logic which is not included under any of the "name" paradoxes and has previously been hinted at rather than formulated precisely. In order to make clear what is meant by an undefined or primitive concept, it is first necessary to provide some form of definition of indefinability in order that these concepts may be distinguished from those which are definable. The definition of indefinability is as valid a form of definition as any other, even though it may be external to the system under discussion. An example occurs in *Principia Mathematica,* p. 93: "If p and q are any propositions, the proposition 'p or q,' i.e. 'either p is true or q is true,' where the alternatives are to be not mutually exclusive, will be represented by '$p \vee q$.'" According to Whitehead and Russell, this is not a definition at all but a primitive idea. It seems to me that this is a nominal definition of their symbol for the primitive idea. The so-called "undefined" ideas of a system must have names and these names must be defined. If they were not defined they would be so unintelligible that nobody would be in a position to say whether they were ultimately definable or not. I submit, therefore, that there is no such thing as an "undefined" concept, since every concept must be capable of nominal definition to be intelligible.

Nominal definitions are necessary not only for the names of primitive ideas but also for those of derived ideas. Another example from the *Principia Mathematica* will be utilized to illustrate this further tenet. Whitehead and Russell use the horseshoe symbol for a derived idea, obtained from the primitive ideas of negation and disjunction by the definition: $p \supset q \cdot = \cdot \sim p \vee q$. Df. If the authors had left their explanation there, it would be possible to argue that, since the derived ideas in an exposition are all analysed into the primitive ideas, the statement of their analysis must serve also as an explanation of the meaning of the names for them. The analysis of the thing and the definition of the name of the thing could be surely considered as the same operation by the analytic method. The nominal definition of the horseshoe symbol could be given by the analysis of the idea of the horseshoe into a certain function of the primitive concepts of negation and disjunction.

The authors did, in fact, not leave their explanation at that point, but coupled the horseshoe symbol with the word "implies." Their further remarks are tantamount to another definition of the horseshoe symbol, viz.:

$$p \supset q \cdot = \cdot p \text{ implies } q.$$

This was necessary if their formal definition was to contain "an analysis of a common idea," for no analysandum would be introduced by the horseshoe symbol without the word "implies." It would only have been a label for the idea "either p is false or q is true." I take it therefore that if the formal definitions in any system are not to be merely abbreviations but are to analyse ideas, there must also be nominal definitions for both primitive and derived ideas.

Though I admit that definitions are necessary in symbolic logic, it does not follow that the general notion of definability as applied to entities in a formal system is itself definable in this system. To demonstrate this we shall presume a formal system S, consistent and similar to that of *Principia Mathematica*. S is based on the simple theory of types, and each variable in S has a definite order. The range of variables of the zeroth order is the set of all natural numbers; variables of the first order represent real numbers, represented by sets of natural numbers[4]; variables of the second order represent sets of real numbers. The constants in S include the customary sentential connectives, the universal quantifier "A," and the identity symbol "=." Entities represented by variables of the nth order are referred to as elements of the nth order.

The data are an element a of the nth order and a formula ϕ in

S which contains a certain nth order variable as the only free variable. The question arises as to whether or not a satisfies ϕ. If a does indeed satisfy ϕ we may say that ϕ defines a provided that no other element satisfies ϕ. The element a is definable in S if there is a formula ϕ in S which defines a. Two examples will augment this reasoning. If "p" and "q" are variables of the zeroth order the formula:

$$A_q\ p + q = q$$

defines the number O. Under the same conditions the formula:

$$A_q\ p \cdot q = q$$

defines the number 1.

This definition can be replaced if a is a set of all elements satisfying a formula ψ which contains a certain variable of the $(n-1)$st order as the only free variable. a is definable in S if there is a formula ψ in S which defines it. A binary relation R is definable if there is a formula containing two different free variables and is satisfied by those ordered couples of elements between which R holds, and by no other couples of elements. With this definition of definability we may discuss the definability of a set a or a relation R in a formal system S_1, even though neither a nor R belongs to the range of any variable occurring in S_1. It is sufficient to assume that all elements of a belong to the range of a variable in S_1, or that all elements of the domain of R belong to the range of a variable in S_1, all elements of the counter-domain of R belonging to the range of any variable in S_1.

We shall denote by "T_n" the set of all elements of the nth order definable in S. The problem under discussion may then be couched succinctly. Is the set T_n a member of the set T_{n+1}? There are only three possible answers:

    a. If $n = 0$, the answer is positive.
    b. If $n = 2$, the answer is negative.
    c. If $n = 1$, the answer is open.

Since every natural number is definable in S, the set T_0 of all natural numbers definable in S is the set of all natural numbers. The positive answer is trivial, but the other two are most interesting.

In discussing answer b we recall that the elements of the second order are sets of real numbers. A one-to-one correspondence may be established between all real numbers and all sets of rational numbers. A well-ordered relation R may be defined whose field consists of sets of real numbers and is non-denumerable. A real number a is well-ordered if the correlated set $\bar{a}$ of rational numbers is well-ordered by the $\leqq$ relation. Two real numbers a and b are similar if the correlated sets $\bar{a}$ and b are ordered similarly. We consider sets of real numbers every one of which consists of all real numbers similar to a well-ordered real number. Let R be the relation which holds between two such sets p and q if and only if there are two real numbers a in p and b in q such that the correlated set $\bar{a}$ of rationals is set-theoretically included in the correlated set of $\bar{i}$ of rationals. The relation R thus defined is a well-ordered relation between sets of real numbers and the field of R is non-denumerable. The relation R is definable in S since the system S provides adequate devices for the formalization of all classical mathematics. A formula in S can be constructed which contains two different variables of the second order, e.g. p and q, as the only free variables and which is satisfied by all those couples of sets p and q of real numbers between which R holds, and only by those couples of sets. This formula may be constructed without using any variable of an order higher than 1 as a bound variable, and may be represented by "$\lambda\ (p, q)$."

The set T_2 of all sets p of real numbers which are definable in S is denumerable since the set of all formulas in S is denumerable. There are sets p of real numbers which belong to the field of R but do not belong to T_2 in virtue of the fact that the field of the relation R is non-denumerable. However, since R is a well-ordered relation, there is a uniquely determined set p_0 of real numbers which belongs to the field of R but not to T_2, and which is in the relation R to any other set q of real numbers belonging to the field of R but not to T_2. Let us assume that the set T_2 is definable in S. Thus, there is a formula in S which contains a variable of the second order, e.g. "p," as the only free variable and which is satisfied by all sets belonging to T_2 and by nothing else. This formula may be symbolized as "$\delta(p)$."

In the following formula ϕ:

$$\lambda(p, p) \cdot \frown \delta(p) \cdot A_q[\lambda(q, q) \cdot \sim \delta(q) \supset \lambda(p, q)],$$

"$\delta(q)$" denotes the formula obtained from "$\delta(p)$" by changing "p" to "q" everywhere. "p" and "q" may be presumed not to occur in "$\delta(p)$" as bound variables. The same procedure holds good for "$\lambda(p, p)$" and "$\lambda(q, q)$." Thus we see that ϕ is a formula in S containing "p" as the only free variable and that the set p_0 previously determined is the only set which satisfies ϕ. Hence ϕ defines p_0 and p_0 is a set of real numbers definable in S. This leads to a contradiction: p_0 both belongs and does not belong to T_2. Therefore we must reject the assumption that T_2 is definable in S. Our answer is thus negative for $n = 2$ and for every natural number in general $n \geqq 2$.

We now turn to answer c. The argument for $n = 2$ manifests that a function f can be constructed correlating, with every denumerable set a of sets of real numbers, a set $f(a)$ of real numbers which does not belong to a. But there is no method of ascertaining whether a function with an analogous property can be defined for denumerable sets of real numbers. It also seems doubtful whether it will ever be possible to construct a well-ordered relation of real numbers with a non-denumerable field. The question whether the notion of a real number definable in a formal system S is itself definable in S remains open and unanswered.

That so many questions of general mathematical definition, such as those just discussed, remain unanswered is to some extent due to the fact that philosophers are by no means decided on the question of the interpretation of mathematics. Thus the proposition:

$$7 + 5 = 12$$

has been taken by Kant as synthetic and by Ayer[5] as tautologous or analytic. There are five symbols here to be interpreted. If the numbers seven, five and twelve are regarded on the basis of the Frege-Russell theory as the names of certain classes, how can we define exactly the significance of plus and minus? Strictly speaking cardinal numbers are independent of one another, as Cassirer[6] has observed. If, as he suggests, we group meat and cherries together under the attributes "red, juicy and edible," we do not obtain a concept of any value whatever. Why do we therefore group together a couple of apricots, twins and a pair of shoes under the general concept "two?" The answer that is usually given, namely that the concept is an open one and must be obtained by the combination of all conceivable dyads, is hardly satisfactory as it implies an infinite process. Nobody has finally decided the question of whether infinite processes can be validly subjected to logical analysis, which is, of course, finite. Until this problem is solved we cannot say for certain whether Ayer's description of mathematics as a vast system of tautology is correct or not.

I do believe that a helpful step is to attempt the reinterpretation of number as an infinite series generated from a primary operation "plus one" by successive iteration. In this way, each positive integer may be shown to be an operation involving the repetition of operation "plus one" according to a pattern which may be integrated with a given master pattern. Seven may then be tentatively interpreted as the operation "plus seven" which is equivalent to the master pattern "$+ 1 + 1 + 1 + 1 + 1 + 1 + 1$." Five and twelve may be similarly regarded. The proposition:

$$7 + 5 = 12$$

may then be described as the combination of the operations

"plus seven" and "plus five" in a manner which formally resembles the operation of repetition of "plus one" and provides the equivalence "plus twelve." From this point of view the property of numbers as expounded by Kant is not necessarily tautological or analytic.

Ayer would doubtless object to this suggestion and I suspect that he would do so by proposing the view that "7 + 5" and "12" are two different names for the same concept. I quote his own words:

"We see, then, that there is nothing mysterious about the apodeictic certainty of logic and mathematics. Our knowledge that no observation can ever confute the proposition '7 + 5 = 12' depends simply on the fact that the symbolic expression '7 + 5' is synonymous with '12,' just as our knowledge that every oculist is an eye-doctor depends on the fact that the symbol 'eye-doctor' is synonymous with 'oculist.' And the same explanation holds for every other *a priori* truth."[7]

This "linguistic" interpretation seems to me to reduce the whole of mathematics to an infinitely extended series of synonyms for isolated concepts. Repeatedly Ayer has maintained the view that "*a priori* propositions tell us nothing except about our use of language." He is right, I believe, in maintaining that the proposition

"If *A* equals *B* then *B* equals *A*"

is not established by sense-observation, yet surely it is clear that it does not assert a determination to use the word "equals" in a certain way. It records that equality is a reciprocal relation by whatever symbol it is represented. Whilst Ayer expounds his standpoint, he also accepts the Russellian reduction of all *a priori* inference to apprehension of the formal relations of classes. But these relationships must be independent of and unaffected by the symbols that are used for "all," "or," "not" and similar words. To interpret mathematics by this method seems to me as valid as to suppose that what happens to a man who lies down in the road in front of an oncoming motor car is due to the fact that he calls it an "automobile."

Purely linguistic procedures can hardly be considered sufficient for an adequate interpretation of mathematics or as a basis for mathematical definition. If definitions are not superfluous in mathematics, their bases should surely be mathematical. Symbolic logic is partly a development of what may be called the analytic aspect of mathematics. But from an aesthetic point of view, quite apart from any other, Kant was indeed justified in emphasizing the role of construction in mathematics and especially the figure in geometrical proof, in order to show that the discipline is synthetic. Perhaps it is not too much to hope that a synthesis of the two viewpoints may eventually be achieved.

NOTES

1. Whitehead, A. N., and Russell, B.: *Principia Mathematica,* Cambridge, 1935. Vol. I, pp. 11–12.
2. Tarski, A.: *Der Wahrheitsbegriff in den formalisierten Sprachen,* in *Studia Philosophica* I, 1935, p. 265.
3. Tarski, A.: *Einige methodologische Untersuchungen über die Definierbarkeit der Begriffe,* in *Erkenntnis,* V, 1935.
4. Definability as applied to sets of real numbers is discussed in: Tarski, A.: *Sur les ensembles définissables de nombres réels* I, in *Fundamenta Mathematicae,* XVII, 1931, pp. 210–239.
5. Ayer, A. J.: "Language, Truth and Logic," London, 1948.
6. Cassirer, E.: "Substance and Function," Chicago, 1923.
7. Ayer, A. J.: *Op. cit.,* p. 85.

The Nature of Probability Statements

THE various conceptions of probability have been classified in three groups by Nagel,[1] the differentiation being this:

1. The classical conception, e.g. that of Bernoulli[2] and Laplace.[3] By these authors probability is defined as the ratio of the number of favorable cases to the number of all possible cases.
2. Relative frequency, the view of Mises,[4] Reichenbach[5] and most modern statisticians.
3. An objective logical relation between propositions, the view of Keynes[6] and Jeffreys.[7]

One important criticism of this division is that it is composed in terms of explicata, and not explicanda, or to put it in other words, the distinction is drawn between the solutions offered by these various theorists, rather than between the problems that each was trying to solve. Carnap[8] has postulated that the number of explicanda seem to be basically two: degree of confirmation (probability$_1$), and relative frequency in the long run (probability$_2$). He has further subdivided the first group of explicanda into three sub-concepts of confirmation: classificatory, comparative and quantitative. These categories will be outlined separately.

The classificatory concept of confirmation is the relation between two sentences, one of which is an observational report and the other a statement about an unknown state of affairs. Neither of these sentences is necessarily similar to the other. Thus the first may contain references to states of affairs not yet known but only assumed, and the second may be a law or any other hypothesis. The forms of the two sentences, m and n, are usually expressed in some way as:

"m is supported by n"
"m is confirmed by n"
"n gives positive or corroborating evidence of m."

And so forth. This concept of confirmation is quite clearly a relationship between two sentences rather than a property of one of them.

The comparative concept of confirmation is usually expressed as a tetradic relation between four sentences, in a form such as this:

"m is more strongly confirmed (supported, etc.) by n than m^1 by n^1."

This may also be a dyadic relation between two pairs of sentences m, n and m^1, n^1. The hypotheses m and m^1 are different from one another, as also are the bodies of evidence n and n^1.

The quantitative concept of confirmation is usually expressed by sentences of this form:

"m is confirmed by n to the degree p."

A good deal of discussion has taken place as to whether a concept of this type ever occurs in the normal converse of a scientist in a natural language. I admit for the present purpose the theoretical possibility of its existence in natural languages and its real existence in formalized languages.

I take it that probability statements may be categorized on the basis of the distinction between probability$_1$ and probability$_2$. I shall generally refer to these two categories as inductive statements and frequency statements respectively. I shall also presume that these two sets of statements have a mathematical calculus in common to a certain extent, but differ in interpretation.

The principal differences which I recognize between inductive statements and frequency statements are set out in the table below.

TABLE COMPARING INDUCTIVE AND FREQUENCY PROBABILITY STATEMENTS

INDUCTIVE STATEMENT	FREQUENCY STATEMENT
1. Probability is assigned to a statement (i.e. a hypothesis) relative to another statement (i.e. the evidence).	Probability is assigned to a class of events (i.e. as a property) relative to another class (i.e. the reference class).
2. Analytic	Synthetic
3. L-true	L-indeterminate
4. Do not usually specify numerical values.	Usually specify numerical values.
5. Established by logical analysis.	Established by empirical procedures.

The fundamental relation between inductive probability and frequency probability I take to be a special instance of the logical relation which generally holds between an empirical, quantitative concept and the corresponding inductive logical concept of its estimate with respect to given evidence. In other words, inductive probability may in certain cases be regarded as an estimate of frequency probability. The relation between the two may be further elucidated by analyzing the meaning of the customary references to what are sometimes called unknown probabilities. At a given time we may not know the value of a certain case of frequency probability in the sense that we do not possess sufficient factual information for its calculation. On the other hand, the value of a case of logical probability for two given sentences cannot be unknown in the same sense. It may be unknown in the sense that a particular logico-mathematical procedure is as yet unaccomplished, but this is an entirely different situation. Sometimes Bernoulli and Laplace refer to unknown probabilities or to the probability of certain probability values, and these formulations have found their way into several statements of Bayes' theorem. These are not valid cases of inductive probability. Since a frequency probability value for any given case is a physical fact, we may inquire about the inductive probability of a particular frequency probability, given the relevant evidence. However, the inquiry would be as pointless as asking about the inductive probability of the statement that $3 + 3 = 6$ or that $3 + 4 = 10$. An inductive probability statement is either L-true or L-false, and is in this respect exactly like an arithmetical statement. Its probability with respect to any evidence is either 1 or 0.

There is yet another relation between inductive probability and frequency probability. Both concepts may be represented as quotients of measures of particular classes and as expressing a numerical ratio for the partial inclusion of one class in another. For frequency probability, the classes are generally determined by factual properties, and their value is found empirically. For logical probability, the classes are ranges of sentences and their value is determined logically.

It has been argued from time to time, and most recently by Reichenbach, that relative frequency probability may be generally formulated in terms of inductive probability. Bernoulli's theorem demonstrates that the value of the relative frequency will remain within prescribed limits, under certain conditions, when the sequence is continued indefinitely. From these positions it has been concluded that frequency acquires a predictive character.

In discussing this viewpoint, it is important to bear in mind that whenever a mathematical theorem such as Bernoulli's is applied, this procedure necessarily involves an additional hypothesis dealing with facts. It is obviously an assumption to maintain that any actual sequence of events can be so described or that the mathematical formulae are invariably applicable. A statement interpreted as a frequency statement cannot possibly be a pure frequency statement when it is taken as holding for the unobserved continuation of the sequence. What it does is to incorporate the prediction in the form of a hypothesis that the observed frequency will continue in the actual future sequence consistently, and to manifest the concept of frequency probability as being inapplicable to prediction without the prior supposition of induction.

Reichenbach's postulation hardly seems to answer this objection. His theory of the inductive conception of probability presupposes that the existence of a limit must be formulated as a fundamental principle of induction, and that a necessary condition of predictability is the ability to apply inductive method in the first instance. The definition of predictability as including a postulation of the existence of certain series having a frequency limit is virtually inclusive of a prescription that nature must possess a certain property. This is not so much a definition as an ontological assumption. It is useless to say that those events are predictable whose sequence has a certain property, for we might wish to predict this very property. I believe that induction should not be regarded as a quest for suitable causal sequences but rather as a logical method of confirming statements about such sequences.

There is no circumstance under which the future continuation of an actual sequence can ever follow a mathematical law, as Bernoulli intimated that it could, even if the frequency in the observed segment of this sequence is consistent. Statements based on the Bernoullian principle are conjectural and not predictive. The inductive conception of such a statement achieves prediction only at the cost of prescription. Bernoulli's theorem is subject to most of the criticism that has been levelled against the classical conception of probability in general and particularly against its premise that inductive inference leads from limited evidence to a more comprehensive hypothesis by the Principle of Induction. When used as a principle based on this premise, Bernoulli's theorem becomes a synthetic statement, since it claims to say something about future events. Induction thus becomes an illegitimate deductive inference masquerading as a mathematical theorem. If the concept of relative frequency is used for induction and prediction, it requires an additional hypothesis to guarantee the consistency and stability of the frequency, and this in its turn changes the character of the probability statement. A pure frequency statement must be descriptive.

Unfortunately, the distinction between degree of confirmation and relative frequency does not finally decide the issue between the a priorist and the frequentist as to the nature of probability. Carnap's definition of probability may be regarded as resting on the distinction between the two given explicanda, degree of confirmation and relative frequency. If probability in the sense of degree of confirmation is defined in terms of this sense alone, it is a necessary feature of the resultant definition that it leaves undecided for some philosophers the question whether a sentence about probability is analytic or synthetic. Carnap's standpoint is that a simple sentence about probability as degree of confirmation is analytic and that a simple sentence about probability as relative frequency is synthetic. Burks[9] has protested that probability in inductive arguments is never used in the first sense in such a way that arguments about it are analytically true or false. The frequentist does not deny that the a priorist thinks he uses the terms in this sense, but maintains that the a priorist thinks this and is mistaken. Peirce applied the concept of relative frequencies to inductive arguments, but rejected the a priorist's procedure of counting logically possible universes. This he said was irrelevant because universes are not as plentiful as blackberries. Even so, it is perfectly possible for the frequentist to accept the calculus of the a priorist as a valid mathematical system without being committed to his semantical distinctions.

It is possible to extend speculation further, and presume, with Hume, that the concomitance of A and B on one or more occasions never gives any valid guarantee that A will be accompanied by B on any subsequent occasion. In other words, probability cannot possibly have any meaning or any existence. We may accept it with an act of faith, but then it becomes an area of metaphysics, and not a part of logic at all.

Keynes[10] took Hume's position seriously, and proceeded to reinstate the existence of probability by his hypothesis of limited independent variety in nature, which provided an initial prior probability for empirical propositions. This stand was countered later by Nicod[11] as not being sufficiently comprehensive to fulfill its own requirements.

The most important suggestion of Jeffreys was that initial prior probability rests on the basis of simple rather than complex laws, though it seems to me invalid to maintain an *a priori* preference for simplicity. Jeffreys' case is fundamentally that of a scientific pragmatist: scientists prefer a simple to a complex law, other things being equal, and scientists have achieved valid results. The entire theory of induction is affected by this, and requires investigation in connection with the validity of experience.

Broadly speaking, the principle of experience, as expounded by Locke, maintains that because things have happened in a certain way in the past, that they will probably happen again in a similar fashion in the future. To illustrate this, we may assume that a sentient being moves along a path of uniform texture and has no knowledge whatever of its length. It does not matter in what the uniformity consists—color, roughness, hardness, etc., would all be acceptable criteria of uniformity. His memory about his progress is valid, and he has an accurate time sense, though this argument would also hold good even if his time sense were rough. He has an enquiring mind, and asks himself ceaselessly whether the path will continue into the future for at least $\frac{1}{x}$ of its past length. He always answers this question in the affirmative, and his answers are correct x times for every once that they are wrong. We may then stipulate the existence of an absolutely precise probability in connection with his af-firmative answers, namely $\dfrac{x}{x+1}$.

It seems reasonable to rely on the principle of experience for the probability of predictions with the proviso that the length of extrapolation is small in relation to the length of the experience. But inevitably the precision of this type of probability rests on the assumption that the affirmation is made continually from the beginning. No definite assertion can be made about answers that are only made now and again. What can be done in this latter case is to surmise the same traveller having a large number of experiences of proceeding along different paths of unknown lengths and inquiring as to the length of the path periodically. If the number of inquiries is sufficiently large, they will be dispersed equi-proportionately with reference to their positions on the different paths. The ratio of $\dfrac{x}{x+1}$ will measure exactly the ratio r of the number of correct answers to the total number of answers. While it is obvious that no traveller can possibly know the value of his own r, the average of all values for r for all travellers can be computed. It is $\dfrac{x^2}{(x+1)^2}$, and constitutes a basic formula of primitive induction.

The principle underlying this formula is the same as that which argues that if a coin is tossed a large number of times it will land on each side an approximately equal number of times. But this does not definitely prove the existence of any law of probability. It may well prove the absence of a specific law governing the appearance of one side or the other. The fact that the coin lands on each side an approximately equal number of times may prove to be merely a residual case where there is no specific law.

One feels equally sceptical about the frequentist position, which is sometimes called the Principle of Non-Sufficient Reason. This maintains that if there are y alternatives, one of which

must be true but about which there is no information whatsoever
as to their respective truth, there is a probability of $\dfrac{1}{y}$ that each
is true. In order to prove this by seeing which alternative be
true on a large number of occasions, it would first of all be necessary to arrange all of a great number of different sets of the alternatives in a serial order, and this is quite obviously impossible
in numerous cases.

At this stage one may reasonably wonder whether it is possible to make any valid presuppositions with reference to probability. Let us suppose that a man M usually decides his actions
in accordance with what seem the probabilities of relevant predictions regarding the observational evidence available to him.
Can this be formally justified, or is it simply a form of supersti-
tion?

We shall presume that M, standing in his doorway one evening, would like to know the probable answer to the question:

"Will the sun shine tomorrow?"

For the previous three evenings there has been a red sky and
sun on the following day. He may conclude that his betting quotient is ¾ in regard to the same event reoccurring. If he makes
a sufficiently long series of conclusions of this type, say once
a week for six months, he may also decide that his predictions
will have a balance of validity where the betting quotient is
never higher than the probability for the prediction in question.

The difficulty seems to be that M's decisions are not logically
necessary but depend on the contingency of facts. M's decisions
would be true if the world as a whole had a uniformity such that
events which occurred frequently in the past under given conditions could be said to occur frequently in the future under the
same conditions. Philosophers have noted the occurrence of
what is sometimes loosely called the Law of Averages, based on
the supposition that a sequence of events which has occurred in
the past under certain conditions may occur under the same conditions in the future *mutatis mutandis*. From this premise some

philosophers have further concluded that the assumption of the uniformity of the world is a necessary presupposition for the validity of inductive or probability inferences. Hence arises a basic justification for applying the inductive method in the determination of general issues. The general statement of this position is sometimes expressed in the Principle of Uniformity.

There are several formulations of the Principle of Uniformity, but three are of especial interest for the present purpose. These are stated in full:

1. The world is uniform.
2. The degree of uniformity of the world is high.
3. If the relative frequency of a property in a long initial segment of a series is high, it will be approximately as high in a sufficiently long continuation of the series.

Hume argued that there is nothing in the idea of past uniformities which implies that these uniformities must continue. From this he concluded that there is no evidence for the Principle of Induction, probability statements being synthetic and not analytic. Those who have followed Hume, using the initial evidence of uniformities, have regarded probability statements as being predictive, and on this basis Hume's scepticism appears irrefutable.

I believe that it is possible to answer Hume's challenge by showing that probability statements are non-predictive, and analytically derivable from statements describing past facts. Let us consider any predictive statement S which says that a certain event e will have a certain characteristic c. On certain data, S has a probability of, say a/b. The question now arises as to the meaningfulness of the general statement.

According to Carnap's definition of probability$_2$, which seems in most respects synonymous with what Lewis[12] calls the "expectation co-efficient," the statement that ec has a probability of a/b is really a statement about a frequency, subject to confirmation or disconfirmation by observation. Lewis, on the other hand, argues that the frequency statement which is equivalent to the original probability statement is not the empirical statement:

"The frequency of c's among the x's actually is a/b,"

but rather:

"The frenquency of c's among the x's is, on data D, validly estimated to be a/b."

This latter statement is held by Lewis to be analytic, given the data on which it is based and the rules of probability inference.

Working on the basis of Carnap's view that probability₂ statements are to be translated into predictive frequency statements, it becomes apparent that no such statement can be more than partially credible. The most that is possible is to form an estimation, on the basis of past experience, that there exists a probability to some degree that the frequency estimate a/b is correct. Furthermore, we are in doubt as to whether the "validly estimated" process is itself valid or not. Given the data, the estimate is surely valid, provided only that the correct rules of inference have been followed. We do not know how good the data are upon which the estimate is made. By Lewis's procedure it would be true to say that a valid estimate based on a large sample is a better estimate than one based on a small sample, a statement which is not universally valid.

Obviously not all probability statements are predictive, for nobody, including professional prophets, knows all predicted facts with certainty. The only plausible claim would be that we know what they are, i.e., we know a probability. But to know a probability is to predict correctly some of a total number of future events. These events could be known only with probability, i.e., in terms of knowledge of some still further future events, themselves known only with probability, and so on. On this interpretation, to know a probability would involve an infinite regress.

If probability statements are to have any plausibility, they cannot be interpreted as asserting facts of a sort which can them-

selves only be known with probability. They must be interpreted
as asserting facts which are known with certainty on the basis of
data already available. Thus the statement:

"On data D, S has probability a/b"

must be analytic and cannot possibly be predictive. Insofar as
it asserts the data D it has empirical content, but all it asserts in
addition to the data is a probability which is analytically derivable from the data by the rules of the evidence. It predicts
nothing, and therefore no future event can be relevant to its
truth. It is true, in all relevant respects, in the same way that the
following statement is true:

"Given that I drink six plus six cups of coffee per week,
then I drink eight plus four cups of coffee per week."

My argument bears a certain similarity to Lewis's well-known
argument of infinite regress, but I differ from his position in two
respects. First, I cannot see any objection to treating expectation
coefficients as empirical statements, provided that reliability
judgments are first considered analytic. Secondly, I cannot agree
that the infinite regress occurs in construing the meaning of
probability judgments in accordance with an empirical interpretation. If the empiricist makes a statement such as this:

" 'S is probable at the degree Z' means that the limit of
frequency is Z,"

no regress is involved. The regress occurs when he is attempting
to answer the question:

"How do you know that Z is what the limit is?"

When asked this question, the empiricist can only proceed after
one of three assertions:

1. He is a total sceptic, i.e., makes no claim to knowledge.
2. He knows the empirical frequency limit with certainty, i.e.,
   makes an implausible claim to knowledge.
3. In knowing a degree-of-confirmation statement, what he

knows is its degree of confirmation, etc. ad infinitum, i.e., involves himself in an infinite series of claims.

This constitutes an impasse in most cases.

It may be helpful at this stage to relate the Principle of Uniformity to probability statements in general. The Principle of Induction itself is a probability statement embodying the Principle of Uniformity. It says that, given past uniformities, it is more probable than not that these uniformities will continue, a statement which follows analytically from past uniformities. The statement that it is highly probable that a certain specific uniformity will continue may be interpreted as meaning that this uniformity has been uniformly observed to hold in the relevant parts of past experience. The statement that future experience as a whole will most probably manifest a certain degree of uniformity may be interpreted as meaning that past experience has uniformly manifested this degree of uniformity over a long period of time.

The Principle of Induction is true of all universes where there are any past uniformities to apply it to. In any such universe, it is probable that past uniformities have continued, i.e., that past uniformities will continue. This is true whatever actual disuniformity in the universe may later become apparent.

It should not be assumed that "if uniformities in the past, then probably the same uniformities in the future" is necessarily implied by "if uniformities in the past then uniformities in the past," since this issue can only be decided with reference to a further sense of probability which Lewis calls P-probably. He claims that to assert the analytic statement "On data D, P (an empirical belief) is probable" is not the same as to assert the predictive statement P-probably. Moore[13] suggests that Lewis's conclusion is that induction must be assumed. The purpose of this is not primarily to justify "P is probable" but to correct "P is probable," which constitutes the evidence, with "P-probably," which constitutes the empirical prediction. Lewis himself confesses that the sense of P-probably is as ineffable and as irreducible as the sense of futurity itself. I strongly suspect that P-probably is a psychologism, though Lewis never gives any indication of this. There is no such thing as an epistemological justification of a state of uncertainty, any more than there is an epistemological justification for making inferences from the observed to the unobserved. But there are casual explanations and epistemological justifications of those mental states and habits which are sometimes expressed by the term "probably." It is in this area of psychologistics that I believe the answer to Lewis's unsolved problem is to be found.

We are now in a position to appreciate more fully the differences in the meaning of probability statements according as they are classed under the categories of probability$_1$ or probability$_2$. Probability$_1$ is a logical property, or two-term relation, attributed to one statement with respect to another statement within a language system. The statement:

$$\text{"bc } (h, e) = d\text{"}$$

means that the hypothesis h is confirmed by the evidence e to the degree d. Probability$_2$, on the other hand, is a physical property, or two-term relation, attributed to an event sequence with respect to another such sequence. The statement:

$$\text{"b}(p, s) = rf\text{"}$$

means that the property p occurs within a sequence s with the relative frequency rf. Statements about probability$_1$ are concerned with hypothesis about physical events and judgments about this hypothesis. They estimate the occurrence of a property or an event relative to known instances of occurrence. Statements about probability$_2$ are concerned with the physical properties of sequences of physical events, and are based ultimately on the fact that probability$_2$ is a physical property of events. Probability$_1$, on the other hand, is a semantical property of statements.

It does not follow, as has sometimes been claimed[14], that probability$_1$ is a semantical version of probability$_2$. This argument, which is worthy of discussion, is sometimes interpreted to mean that by translating the probability of events one obtains the probability of a hypothesis. Three principal difficulties are involved.

First, if we replace a physical event by its name, what we do is to erect an entirely different series of events, in this case a series of letter-designs, which is obviously not needed. Letter-design frequency is not truth frequency, and individual names do not represent the truth of specific statements. Truth is not a thing and it cannot be counted.

Secondly, this argument has involved the application of the concept of probability$_2$ to single cases. This procedure I believe erroneous for three reasons:

1. By its own definition this type of probability requires a sequence for it to be existent at all.
2. The sequence must possess a limit, i.e., a rule of formation for the members of the sequence.
3. The sequence must possess randomness, i.e., general independence among the members.

The presence of the third reason prevents the sequence from being causal or deterministic. If it had either of these characteristics it would obviously not come under the probability category at all. Reichenbach's attempt to apply probability$_2$ to single cases rests on the assumption of a fictitious meaning to the probability statement in question. A posit, i.e. a wager, is made by which a weight is assigned to single events, and this weight is claimed to be the probability of the occurrence of single events. This is tantamount to introducing probability$_1$ to save the situation. The very fact that the probability has to be estimated on the basis of statistical evidence manifests that we are no longer dealing with a pure frequency concept. The term "posit" implies the estimation of value, and an estimated value need not be the actual value. A frequency statement applied to a single case is without meaning and incompatible with its own definition.

Thirdly, it is not always clear in the formulation of probability statements whether the meaning should refer to a class or a class of classes, to a sequence or a sequence of sequences. The statement:

"The probability of being given a particular card from a pack is 1/52"

clearly refers to a property of an event-sequence. A property of a frequency-sequence is manifested in this analogous statement:

"The probability of obtaining a probability of 1/52 in being given a particular card from a pack is virtually 1."

The grammarians shudder at sentences which introduce the notion that "it is probable that the probability . . ." but such clauses are essential in clarifying this overlap in probability theory. The frequency-sequence mentioned in the above statement may itself be a sequence selected from the main event-sequence, and as such is a relative frequency. It is sometimes referred to as a "higher-order probability" and covers the frequency in finite segments of the main event-sequence. The term "higher level probability" was used by Reichenbach to cover infinite frequency-sequences. When each frequency is obtained from an infinite event-sequence, all the sub-sequences are independent of one another. His theory of probability-lattices and of the hierarchy of posits makes the whole of induction rest on the convergence of series of higher level. Statistical textbooks tended in the past to treat event-distribution and frequency-distribution as if there were no substantial difference between them, thus adding to the general confusion.

This standpoint has been challenged on several occasions, e.g. by Kneale[15] and Hutten.[16] The latter has rightly pointed out that a sentence commencing with "The probability of the probability . . ." cannot be synonymous with "It is probable that the probability . . ." Similarly a class of classes is not equivalent to a statement about a class, nor is a sequence of sequences equivalent to a statement about a sequence, any more than a sentential junction is the same as a sentential proposition. If inductive probability statements were empirical, there would inevitably be an infinite regress in inductive method—a consequence which is generally admitted among frequency theorists. The conclusion of an inductive inference cannot necessarily be proved to be either true or probable, and so must be analytic. But the empirical character of inductive probability statements implies that the rules of inductive inference must be used as synthetic sentences, a state of affairs which is clearly contradictory. It either takes for granted assumptions about the world or prescribes the course of nature or does both. Unless the statements stating the conclusion of an inductive inference are analytic, there would seem to be no logical procedure for constructing any system of inductive methodology.

A systematic examination of the nature of inductive inference has been provided by Kaufmann,[17] and rests largely on the basis of a dichotomy between "accepted" and "unaccepted" propositions. A "sharp line of demarcation" is drawn "by distinguishing the status of propositions which makes them eligible for the function of grounds in an inductive inference from the status which excludes them from this function." He does not reject the distinction between more or less firmly established propositions and admits that it is essential in any analysis of scientific procedure, but this distinction presupposes the basic dichotomy between accepted and unaccepted propositions.

That statements should, in general, be thus divided seems to me unnecessary. Let us suppose that a man M sees another man M_1 and makes a statement S describing M_1, which he considers possibly certain rather than probably certain, i.e. he makes a distinction between more or less firmly established propositions. In determining the degree of confirmation of two hypotheses H_1 and H_2, he includes S into his consideration of H_1, but not of H_2. But it does not follow that S is necessarily acceptable in the first instance and unacceptable in the second. Surely there are degrees of acceptability in situations such as these. In the case of H_1, S may be the least unacceptable of a series of statements, and in the case of H_2, S may be entirely acceptable except for one small detail. Surely a more refined formulation would be to say that M attaches a significant acceptability to S in each case. The task of inductive inference would then be to determine the derivative acceptability of a hypothesis with respect to a class of evidence statements for which the levels of initial significant acceptability are given. Attempts at inductive procedures of this type, though highly complicated, have been made.[18]

In assessing the presuppositions of induction generally, I wish to propose that it is not necessary to jettison empiricism from the theory of probability as so many authors, notably Lord Russell, have done. They argue that the statement of the probability of uniformity is a synthetic factual statement, and cannot be confirmed empirically because such a procedure would use the method of induction which in turn presupposes the statement. But it is surely possible to show that the inductive method, regarded as yielding a fair betting quotient, is valid without abandoning empiricism.

Let us presume that M wishes to discover what kind of assurance justifies his implicit habit or explicit general decision of determining all his specific decisions with the aid of inductive methodology. Of course it is not necessary that he should know with certainty that this procedure will be successful in the long run, but he should have the assurance of probable success in the long run. We suppose that there are three possible statements by which M may predict that the sun will shine tomorrow:

    1. The sun will shine tomorrow.

This is an absolute predictive statement and not a probability statement. It does not therefore come within the scope of the discussion at present.

    2. With reference to the available evidence, the inductive probability that the sun will shine tomorrow is high.

This is sufficient basis for a decision. M then continues to ask himself if he is justified in making this prediction:

3. "If I make a sufficiently long series of bets where the betting quotient is never higher than the inductive probability for the prediction that the sun will shine tomorrow, then my total balance will be a gain."

Obviously the truth of 3 is not logically necessary. Instead of this statement, M can make an inductive statement such as 4 or 5.

4. "If I make a long series of bets such that the betting quotient is never higher than the inductive probability for the prediction that the sun will shine tomorrow, then it is highly probable that my total balance will be a gain."
5. "If I make a long series of bets in the manner described in statement 4, then the estimate of my total balance will be a gain."

The probability of success in the long run seems sufficient for the validity of inductive inference. Certainty of the uniformity of the world is not necessary. We may therefore rephrase the statements 2 and 3 of the Principle of Uniformity given on page 66, by statements 6 and 7 or 8 and 9. The first two formulations are in terms of a probability, the second two in terms of an estimate. Both, I believe, are equally valid.

6. On the basis of the available evidence it is probable that the degree of uniformity of the world is high.
7. On the basis of the evidence that the relative frequency of a property in a long initial segment of a series is high, it is probable that it will be of approximately equal height in a long continuation of the series.
8. On the basis of the available evidence, the estimate of the degree of uniformity of the world is high.
9. On the basis of the evidence that the relative frequency of a property in a long initial segment of a series is high, the

estimate of the relative frequency in a continuation of the series is of approximately equal height.

I differentiate in any inductive statement between the hypotheses involved and the statement of the inductive relation between the hypothesis and the evidence. The statement of the inductive relation is purely logical and, if true, is analytic. This holds good both for statements of the probability of uniformity 6 and 7, and for statements of the estimate of uniformity 8 and 9. Since none of these is L-indeterminate, no empirical confirmation is required.

An apparently persuasive argument against this position would assert that the statement of the probability of uniformity must be taken as an L-indeterminate statement, since if it were not, M would have no assurance of success in the long run. But surely it is not possible to give M any assurance of the sun shining whatsoever, even in the long run. All that M can have is the probability of sunshine as put forward in statement 4. This statement is itself L-true. It may be further objected that an L-true statement which says nothing about the world is hardly sufficient basis for any serious decision procedure. But in fact M has two statements as a basis for decision: an L-indeterminate statement of his own observational evidence and an L-true statement of inductive probability. Admittedly the second statement adds nothing in factual content to the first, but it does clarify the inductive-logical relation between the original hypothesis and the evidence available. This inductive statement was expressed on page 74 as statement 2 for the hypothesis 1. M learns from 2 that the evidence available to him gives more support to his prediction of sunshine tomorrow rather than no sunshine tomorrow. He is then in a position to make practical decisions about his actions on the following day. In general it is reasonable for M to determine all his specific decisions with the help of the inductive method on the basis of the probable uniformity of the world. His success in the long run is probable in view of his evidence, but I do not believe that a stronger statement than this, or one tantamount to complete prediction could be proved valid by purely logical procedures.

It would perhaps appear, at least from an initial impression, that the standpoint which I have adopted is considerably moved from that of Reichenbach, who is one of the greatest of the exponents of frequency probability. But the differences are not fundamental except in a few specific instances. Inductive probability, as I have argued for it, seems in all essential characteristics the same as Reichenbach's conception of "predictional value," especially as Reichenbach augments this term by saying that it is determined not only by the event in question but "also by the state of our knowledge." His procedure of "appraising" necessitates a distinction between the actual value and the appraisal of a magnitude, the latter half of the distinction being virtually an estimate of relative frequency. He takes the case of a wager:

"The man who bets on the outcome of a boxing match, or a horserace, or a scientific investigation . . . makes use of such instinctive appraisals of the weight (i.e. the logical concept of probability); the height of his stakes indicates the weight appraised."

This is an excellent example of Reichenbach's use of the relative frequency procedure. What it means is that the estimation of this relative frequency by the man who bets determines the betting quotient at which he is disposed to make a bet. Reichenbach realizes very rightly that what determines the bettor's decision concerning a betting quotient is not the actual relative frequency in the future (since this is unknown) but the estimate of it. Where Reichenbach errs, it seems to me, is in implying that inductive probability can only be explicated by identifying it with relative frequency itself instead of with an estimate of relative frequency.

Some of the criticisms which Reichenbach makes of the views of Laplace and Keynes are admittedly acceptable, but he does not succeed in invalidating their views, either because of their a priorism or on any other grounds, because he uses one of their basic formulations himself, i.e. the concept of an estimate of relative frequency. Perhaps a justifiable criticism of Reichenbach's position in general is that he did not always pursue his own arguments to their logically possible conclusions. Had he done so, he would surely have arrived at an inductive theory of estimation in connection with his own theory of frequency. Reichenbach also tends to regard inductive probability as having a place in logic superior to that of truth and falsehood, and to view multi-valued probability logic as a better tool than two-valued logic. Part of the difficulty here is the result of the classical connotations of absolute truth which surround the word "true" and blur the distinction between "true" and "known to be true by complete confirmation." The second should be replaced by some phrase such as "inductively true," and judged according to the continuous scale of inductive probability values. By making use of this scale, I do not imply that inductive logic is multi-valued, as Reichenbach suggests. Like deductive logic, it remains two-valued. The dichotomy is not the traditional division into truth and falsehood, but the more recent distinction between L-implication and non-L-implication of two sentences.

Both Reichenbach and Carnap agree that synthetic propositions have no *a priori* status and in most instances I maintain the same position. A recent attempt by Langford[19] to show that synthetic necessary propositions do exist does not seem to substantiate its own claims. Langford's argument is that the proposition

"Any cube has twelve edges"

is both synthetic and *a priori* or necessary. The defence of this position is that the common notion of a cubical object is a purely geometrical idea, so that the property of knowing twelve edges cannot be deduced by means of logical principle alone from the property of being a cube. Since most people do not know how many edges a cube has, and since a person can ascertain this number by finding an object which is cubical and counting its edges, the notion of having twelve edges can be no part of the notion of being a cube, since, if it were, he would then not know what it was the edges of which he was counting.

Langford admits that if the postulates which have to be added to an adequate definition of "cube" in order to derive the geometrical theorem "all cubes have twelve edges" are propositional functions, then it cannot be presumed that this theorem expresses a proposition at all. If the postulates are interpreted in terms of physical space, the theorem may not be *a priori*. But his proof seems rather to show that all theorems which require postulates in addition to their definitions as means of demonstration are synthetic necessary propositions, if we only suppose that they refer to visual space. Fewer thinkers will quarrel with Langford if the argument is confined to his very specialized meaning of *a priori* synthetic propositions.

One further proposition taken from Langford's article may clarify this line of thinking. He offers the proposition

"Whatever is red is colored"

as an example of a synthetic necessary proposition, and maintains that "x is colored" cannot be formally deduced from "x is red" on the grounds that a man who is able to understand the meanings of the extra-logical terms in the premises of a formal argument should also be able to understand the meanings of the extra-logical terms in its conclusion. In a formal argument no new non-logical concepts, which are not present in the premises, can occur in the conclusion. He further argues that a man with monochromatic vision might understand the meaning of "red" without understanding the meaning of "colored." This convinces him that the proposition is synthetic.

The reason that I am not wholly convinced of Langford's argument is that his term "synthetic a priori" seems in some respects a species of analytic proposition. This doubt is enhanced by Langford's description of postulates as implicit definitions of the primitives they contain, and by the lack of a precise extension designated to the term "definition" in the characterization of analytic propositions as propositions demonstrable with the sole help of definitions. But I do believe that Langford's proposition, and similar propositions, may be justified as synthetic and necessary if it is assumed that "red" and "colored" are not logical constants. It is reasonable to suppose that the conditional "if x is red then x is colored" has the form "if P then p or q," because to say "x is colored" is to say "x is green, blue, red or any other color that has received a name." Suppose that every color with a name were actually written out in this last sentence, and that a short time afterwards we discovered an object having an unnamed color. Surely the object would be colored. Yet if colored meant what it had been defined to mean, the object would not be colored. 'Colored,' like 'red,' must therefore be regarded as a term whose meaning is only substantiated by ostensive definition and which belongs to the primitive vocabulary. The argument "x is red, therefore x is colored" would be only formally valid if all arguments of the form "x is P, therefore x is Q" were valid.

In this connection Pap,[20] in defending the existence of synthetic necessary propositions, protests against making the distinction between logical and non-logical expressions an absolute one. If we define a logical expression as an expression that functions logically in the context of an argument in which it occurs, or use Quine's phrase "essential occurrence," the whole question of whether any necessary propositions could fail to be analytic becomes blurred. If we take Pap's suggestion and define "logical principle" more or less arbitrarily by laying down a number of postulates and rules of derivation and then defining "logical principle" as any proposition derivable in this system, including the postulates which are derivable from themselves, then Langford's position seems quite acceptable. Pap's tightly circumscribed conclusion may be irrefutable in the light of his own definition of "logical constant":

"But I see no escape from the conclusion, well worth repeating, that those definitions which syntactically function as rules of translation from one universe of discourse to another, and thus enable incorporation of more and more material into logic, express . . . necessary or *a priori* propositions; and since the necessity of those propositions is the ground that makes those definitions cognitively acceptable, it would be circular to prove that they are analytic by reference to the very definitions which they are to support."[21]

Finally, it is perhaps appropriate to remark that many philosophers, e.g. Keynes and Jeffreys, have not taken sentences as arguments but something described by sentences, e.g. propositions, events, occurrences, etc. These authors consequently write sentences as argument expressions, e.g.:

1. 'The probability that . . . is 1/6.'
2. 'P (a/h) = 1/6.' (Keynes)
3. 'a/h = 1/6.' (Keynes)
4. 'P (q|p) = 1/6.' (Jeffreys)

As a result of this type of formulation, inductive probability is regarded as an intensional function and must, though the authors nowhere say so, be based not on a system of ordinary symbolic logic but on an intensional, modal system. A few authors, e.g. Mazurkiewicz and Hosiasson, have taken arguments as sentences, and have written names of sentences as argument expressions. For this procedure modal logic is not necessary as a basis since the language can be extensional. As well as being relative to the evidence available, inductive probability is also relative to the language system and to semantical L-concepts. It may even be interpreted as a quantitative semantical L-concept. Apart from tentative pronouncements by Carnap,[22] the relations between inductive and semantical procedures have been virtually ignored by writers on probability. It is in this direction that much pioneer research still remains to be executed.

NOTES

1. Nagel, E.: "Principles of the Theory of Probability" in the Introduction to the Encyclopaedia of Unified Science, Vol. I, No. 6. Chicago, 1939.
2. Bernoulli, J.: "*Ars Conjectandi*," Basiliae, 1713.

"Wahrscheinlichkeitsrechnung," (Trans. R. Haussner, 2 vols.; Ostwalds Klassiker), Leipzig, 1899.

3. LaPlace, P. S. de: *"Théorie Analytique des Probabilités,"* Paris, 1812.

4. Mises, R. von: *"Grundlagen der Wahrscheinlichkeitsrechnung,"* in *Math ZS,* vol. 5, 1919, pp. 52–99.
   "Wahrscheinlichkeit, Statistik und Wahrheit," Wein, 1928. Translated as "Probability, Statistics and Truth," New York, 1939.
   "Wahrscheinlichkeitsrechnung und Ihre Anwendung in der Statistik und Theoretischen Physik," Wein, 1931.

5. Reichenbach, H.: "The Logical Foundations of the Concept of Probability" in "Readings in Philosophical Analysis," ed. H. Feigl and W. Sellars, New York, 1949.
   "The Theory of Probability," Berkeley, 1949.

6. Keynes, J. M.: "A Treatise on Probability," London, 1929.

7. Jeffreys, H.: "Scientific Inference," Cambridge, 1931.
   "The Problem of Inference," in *Mind,* Vol. 45, 1936, pp. 324–333.
   "Theory of Probability," Oxford, 1939.

8. Carnap, R.: "Logical Foundations of Probability," Chicago, 1950.

9. Burks, A. W.: Review of "Logical Foundations of Probability" in *Journal of Philosophy,* Vol. XLVIII, No. 17, August 16, 1951, pp. 524–535.

10. Keynes, J. M.: "A Treatise on Probability," London, 1929. Chapter 22.

11. Nicod, J.: "Foundations of Geometry and Induction," London, 1930, pp. 266–281.

12. Lewis, C. I.: "An Analysis of Knowledge and Valuation," LaSalle, 1947.

13. Moore, A.: "The Principle of Induction (II): A Rejoinder to Miss Brodbeck," in *Journal of Philosophy,* Vol. XLIX, No. 24, Nov. 20, 1952.

14. For example, by:
    Reichenbach, H.: See *Journal of Unified Science,* Vol. VIII, 1938.
    Von Wright, G. H.: "The Logical Problem of Induction," Helsinki, 1941.

15. Kneale, W.: "Probability and Induction." Oxford, 1949.

16. Hutten, E. W.: "Probability-Sentences" in *Mind,* Vol. LXI, No. 241, January, 1952.

17. Kaufmann, F.: "Scientific Procedure and Probability," in *Philosophy and Phenomenological Research,* Vol. VI, No. 1, September, 1945.

18. For example:

(1). Helmer, O. and Oppenheim, P.: "A Syntactical Definition of Probability and of Degree of Confirmation," in *Journal of Symbolic Logic*, Vol. X, 1945.

(2). Hempel, C. G. and Oppenheim, P.: "A Definition of 'Degree of Confirmation,' " in *Philosophy of Science*, Vol. XII, 1945.

(3). Hempel, C. G.: "A Purely Syntactical Definition of Confirmation," in *Journal of Symbolic Logic*, Vol. VIII, 1943.

19. Langford, C. H.: "A Proof that Synthetic A Priori Propositions Exist," in *Journal of Philosophy*, Vol. XLVI, No. 1, January 6, 1949.

See also "The Philosophy of G. E. Moore," ed. P. A. Schlipp, "The Library of Living Philosophers," pp. 321 ff.

20. Pap, A.: "Are All Necessary Propositions Analytic?" in *Philosophical Review*, Vol. LVII, July, 1949.

"Logic and the Synthetic A Priori," in *Philosophy and Phenomenological Research*, Vol. X, July, 1950.

21. Pap, A.: Second cited article, p. 514.

22. Carnap, R.: "Logical Foundations of Probability." Chicago, 1950.

The Pragmatic Theory of Truth

I begin by distinguishing between the three very different senses in which Peirce, James and Dewey used the word "Pragmatism." This distinction depends primarily upon the difference between the task of specifying the conditions under which a word or a concept or an idea can be said to have meaning, and the quite different, if closely related, task of specifying the conditions under which a proposition can be said to be true. To offer a rough approximation at the outset: The pragmatic maxim is proposed by Peirce as a rule for the attainment of "clarity of our conceptions," i.e. as a theory of meaning, and is associated with an account of the notion of truth which is not itself appropriately labelled "pragmatic." James stated the principle of pragmatism alternately as a theory of the nature of meaning and the theory of truth. Dewey, more rigorous than James, if less clear, preferred to eliminate the concept of truth. In its stead he substituted a concept of "warranted assertibility," which, in conjunction with Peirce's pragmatic account of meaning, seemed to Dewey an adequate explication of the conditions of successful thinking.

Peirce was himself a physical scientist, and his philosophy is in large degree the result of speculation upon the methods of physical science. There seemed to him to be three major steps involved in scientific method which philosophers would do well to consider. The first is the formulation of hypotheses as the result of observation. A scientist confronted by data does not just stare at them, but formulates an idea or a hypothesis. The second step is the eliciting from the hypothesis of the condition of further experiment. A scientist in possession of a hypothesis does not simply stand in awe of it. He determines the conditions of future observations (i.e. of his experiments) by deducing what further things would be the case if the hypothesis were assumed to be correct. The third step consists in the actual experimenting and the inevitable alteration of the hypothesis in the light of the new data. The three-fold process thus begins again and continues indefinitely.

Peirce, speculating upon this method, came to a great many revolutionary conclusions. But among them are two which are central, and which form the base upon which everything else he said rests.

The first principle is the Principle of Pragmatism. It relates largely to what I have described as the second step of scientific method. Suppose that a scientist is asked to clarify the meaning of any hypothesis or of the concepts contained in it, the only sensible thing he can do is to "elicit from it the conditions of further experiment." When the scientist sets up his experiment and declares from his hypothesis the sensible consequences which would be observed if the hypothesis were correct what he is doing is clarifying the meaning of his hypothesis. This statement is sometimes referred to as the pragmatic criterion: "Consider what effects, that might conceivably have practical bearings, we conceive the object of our conception to have. Then our conception of these effects is the whole of our conception of the object."[1]

Some critics have gone as far as to say that this is the only import of Peirce's pragmatic maxim.Though I admit that this application of the first principle is very important, and that it represents the popular view of Peirce's pragmatism, I believe that Peirce had a much broader application in mind. He aimed primarily at providing a pragmatic criterion of meaning, and it seems to me that this involved fundamentally the meaning of signs. The sign-situation is thus an essential presupposition of pragmatism. Signs surely embrace not only hypotheses but also data, and the pragmatic criterion of meaning, according to Peirce, would seem to be applicable to all synthetic sentences and data as well as hypotheses.

Embodied also in the Principle of Pragmatism is the notion of "abduction," which is not only present in the first steps of scientific method, but exists in observation itself, beforehand. As an ampliative inference it takes this form:

"The surprising fact, C, is observed;
But if A were true, C would be a matter of course,
Hence there is no reason to suspect that A is true."[2]

Perception, or observation is, on this view, a hypothesis, i.e. a judgment inferred abductively. In other words, perception is an interpretation. That abduction is one of the most important features in Peirce's pragmatism is evidenced by his insistence that abduction is the source of new ideas. It is in reconciling the concept of abduction with his previously formulated realism that Peirce parts company with most other pragmatists. Even so it seems to me that Peirce's argument can be accepted as valid if one sees no essential dichotomy between realist and pragmatist interpretations of objective inference.

In tackling this particular question, I find it germane that Peirce adopted two different kinds of statement in explicating his pragmatism. One kind is related to physical science and is in line with his realism, while the other kind is related to practical matters and human conduct, and is much more frequently found in the works of James, Dewey and Mead. In the former kind of statement, examples of which occur throughout Peirce's writings, a term has meaning if and only if it has a "logical interpretant of a certain kind." This interpretant must be a sign of something observable, publicly sensible, and accessible as the result of a specifiable experiment. Thus a term has meaning only as it is a prescription of an act to be performed and a description of a publicly observable result.

The latter kind of statement is exemplified by the following:

". . . the true meaning of any product of the intellect lies in whatever unitary determination it would impart to practical conduct under any and every conceivable circumstance, supposing such conduct to be guided by reflexion carried to an ultimate limit."[3]

The necessary form that gives the meaning of a given proposition is further elaborated:

"It is, according to the pragmaticist, that form in which the proposition becomes applicable to human conduct, not in these or those special circumstances, nor when one entertains this or that special design, but that form which is most directly applicable to self-control under every situation, and to every purpose."[4]

As Buchler[5] has remarked, Peirce probably adopted this latter and vaguer kind of statement through his association with James who used this type of language habitually. Hereby Peirce's pragmatism becomes a much bigger enterprise than he himself had taken it to be. It takes on the characteristics of a doctrine of ethics and of metaphysics not unlike that of Dewey in its fundamental features. It becomes anthropomorphic, though not anthropocentric, in its emphasis on such human manifestations as habits, conduct and self-control. Nobody was more aware than Peirce that the pragmatic criterion has not only to be stated, but also to be justified. This he did, in one way, by showing that pragmatism is a rule which promotes the success of the sign-situation,[6] and in another way by demonstrating that the pragmatic criterion is implicit in the life-process itself.

Peirce was convinced that traditional notions of clarification by definition put, as he liked to say, the cart in front of the horse. One cannot give a clear definition of a concept which is already nebulous. It is essential to clarify meaning prior to formulation of any definition. Peirce formulated his pragmatic maxim in an attempt to get the horse in front of the cart. In doing this he presented the grandfather of most twentieth-century theories of meaning of meaning. Granting that one must clarify meaning in the first place, the critic of pragmatism can and frequently does reply to Peirce that the clarification of meaning presupposes that there already exists an antecedent meaning to clarify. This meaning, the critics have advanced, is logically distinguishable from the meaning as Peirce's pragmatic criterion states it. I quite agree that Peirce's criterion may be modified to meet this objection, but this can be done without surrendering its essential point.

I turn now, however, to the second fundamental principle. This Peirce called the "Principle of Fallibilism," and it relates to a very different feature of the scientific method from that to which the pragmatic maxim relates. It springs from what Peirce held to be the intrinsically directional character of the method. It is an essential presupposition of the method already outlined that the succession of constantly altered hypotheses is both a succession and a progression. That is to say, the whole process will be indulged in only if it is assumed that it is directional. And to Peirce the assumption that a series is directional is equivalent to the assumption that it has an ideal limit, and his term for the ideal limit toward which science must be assumed to be directed is the words "The Truth."

The principle of fallibilism emphasizes that one is never justified in assuming that the latest and best and so-far-uncontroverted hypothesis necessarily is (or accurately expresses) this ideal limit. One must always distinguish the latest and best hypothesis from the Truth which constitutes the ideal limit of the process. The conjunction of these two principles in Peirce underscores as nothing else can the fundamental character of his distinction between the problem of meaning and the problem of truth.

His critics have further stated on occasions that Peirce defined the truth relation in old-fashioned correspondence terms. Though I agree that he was a thorough-going realist, both about things and about concepts, and considered the great question of truth as one of the relation between propositions in our discourse to events occurring independently of that discourse, it seems to me that Peirce's pragmatism prevented his realism from being the old-fashioned correspondence view that some commentators take it to be. Great care needs to be taken in digesting the whole of Peirce's theory of truth, and especially in interpreting the meaning that he attaches to the words "real" and "reality" whenever they appear in his writings. That meaning, I submit, is the pragmatic and not the common realist meaning.

Truth, for Peirce as for realists, has to do with reality and "that is real which has such and such characters, whether anybody thinks it to have those characters or not."[7] While Peirce insists that a true belief corresponds with the real, it is significant that he also claims that truth is always relative to investigation, e.g.: "Reality is only the object of the final opinion to which sufficient investigation would lead."[8] In this vein he speaks of his "social theory of reality,"[9] according to which the concept of reality "involves the notion of a community." The real is "the idea in which the community ultimately settles down." Such pronouncements, and many more like them, show that Peirce was not a realist in any sense opposed to pragmatism. The "real" means nothing save as it is definable experimentally in publicly verifiable operations. Thus Peirce's realism, like that of James and Dewey, is never committed to a reality independent of experience. "The opinion which is fated to be ultimately agreed to by all who investigate, is what we mean by the truth, and the object represented in this opinion is the real. That is the way I would explain reality."[10] And immediately following this Peirce says significantly:

"But it may be said that this view is directly opposed to the abstract definition which we have given of reality [old-fashioned realism], inasmuch as it makes the characters of the real depend on what is ultimately thought about them. But the answer to this is that, on the one hand, reality is independent, not necessarily of thought in general, but only of what you or I or any finite number of men may think about it; and that, on the other hand, though the object of the final opinion depends on what that opinion is, yet what that opinion is does not depend on what you or I or any man thinks."

The basic theories of Peirce are augmented in the work of James, for whom truth is a property of certain of our ideas. Fundamentally, James' position is that truth happens to an idea. Its verity is in fact the process of its verifying itself, i.e. its verification. Its validity is the process of its validation. Verification means the ability to guide us prosperously through experience. The practical value of true ideas is primarily derived from the practical importance of their objects to us. Relations among purely mental ideas form a species of eternal truth, e.g., $1 + 1 = 2$. Beliefs verified concretely by somebody are the posts of the whole superstructure of truth. "To agree" with a reality can only mean to be guided either straight up to it or into its surroundings, or to be put into such working touch with it as to handle either it or something connected with it better than if we disagreed. Agreement is essentially a leading into quarters that contain objects that are important. Truth is a collective name for verification-processes, and is made, just as health and wealth are made, in the course of experience. Truth is good, like health and wealth, and grows continually. We have to live by what truth we can get done today and be ready tomorrow to call it falsehood. Rationalist attempts to explain truth in other ways are "indescribably futile."

Not infrequently James has written accounts of truth which seem to justify the belief that, for him, to be true is more than to be verified. Three examples are the following:[11]

". . . any idea that will carry us prosperously from any one part of our experience to any other part, linking things satisfactorily, working securely, simplifying, saving labor; is true for just so much . . . ." (p. 58)

"Our account of truth is an account of truths in the plural, of processes of leading, realized *in rebus,* and having only this quality in common, that they pay. They pay by guiding us into or towards some part of a system with which at any rate we are now in the kind of commerce vaguely designated as verification." (p. 218)

"The truth of an idea is not a stagnant property inherent in it. Truth *happens* to an idea. It becomes true, is made true by events. Its verity *is* in fact an event, a process: the process namely of its verifying itself, its *verification.*" (p. 201)

If we assume that James is committed to the belief that the true is the same as the verified, serious difficulties are encountered, as his critics have pointed out. There are undoubtedly many statements which never have been and never will be verified or falsified, not because they cannot be but because no one has or will take the trouble to test them. Such statements are, on James's theory, neither true nor false. But this violates a basic rule of language, the law of the excluded middle, which requires that every statement be either true or false. Since the verification-status of a statement may vary at different times—it may be verified or confirmed at one time and falsified or disconfirmed at another—a statement may be true at one time and false at another. This again violates a fundamental rule concerning the use of the word 'true.' A statement cannot be both true and false, according to the law of contradiction. A statement might be warranted, or reasonably well verified, in 1460 and not warranted in 1960; but warrant or credibility is quite different from truth. Truth, in short, is something which a statement either has or does not have once and for all and independently of whether or not it has been or ever will be actually confirmed or disconfirmed by any person. James may very well be explicating the notion of verification in an interesting way but his account is obviously inadequate if taken, as he takes it, as a theory of the nature of truth.

The definition of truth to which James adheres when he is seeking formal rigor is one which identifies truth and verifiability. To say that a belief is true is not to say that it is verified, but to say that it is verifiable. "Verifiable" does not mean here theoretically capable of being either verified or falsified, confirmed or disconfirmed. Perkins[12] has explained it well. The sentence "p is verifiable" means that if p were carefully tested over an indefinitely long period it would be verified or confirmed to any increasingly higher degree. The truth of a belief is in its disposition to be confirmed in the long run and under certain conditions, i.e., if it is carefully tested. It is a potentiality or tendency of the belief or statement to be confirmed eventually if tested; it is not a state of actual confirmation.

Versions of the verifiability view are frequently expressed by James. Thus as early as *Pragmatism* James writes:

"The quality of truth, obtaining *ante rem,* pragmatically means, then, the fact that in such a world innumerable ideas work better by indirect or possible than by their direct and actual verification. Truth *ante rem* means only verifiability...."[13]

And later he writes:

"*What constitutes the relation* known as truth, I now say, is just the *existence in the empirical world of this fundamentum of circumstance surrounding object* and *idea* and ready to be either short-circuited or traversed at full length. So long as it exists, and a satisfactory passage through it between the object and the idea is possible, that idea will both *be* true, and will have been true of that object, whether fully developed verification has taken place or not."[14]

"I myself agree most cordially that for an idea to be true the object must be 'as' the idea declares it, but I explicate the 'as'-ness as meaning the idea's verifiability...."[15]

This conception of truth is free from the criticisms which have been directed at his alleged identification of truth and verification. Verifiability is a property which every statement either definitely has or definitely does not have, regardless of whether it ever has been or will be actually verified. Furthermore it is a property which a statement has once and for all. It is not capable of being confirmed in the indefinitely long run at one time and incapable of such long-run confirmation at another time. The verifiability is a disposition of the statement which exists in the statement initially and permanently, even though it may never show itself in any particular verification if it is never actually tested. It is a dispositional property, such that the laws of contradiction and excluded middle are valid when it is identified with truth.

The most important cause for the failure of James to adhere consistently to expression of the "verifiability" definition is the fact that he was usually trying to forward three different projects at the same time. Two of these frequently interfered with the third. The three endeavors were first, to explain truth in terms of a certain relation of an "idea" to verification, that of ability to be verified; secondly, to develop a new theory of actual verification and hence of knowledge, the "utilitarian" theory; and thirdly, to defend a form of nominalism, insisting upon the analysis of concepts in terms of the *concreta* which alone constitute their ultimate referents. Often he was really concerned with the second and the third while ostensibly attempting the first. This fact explains many of his defections from expression of the verifiability theory of truth.

James's conception of truth contains three elements which call for analysis: the conditional form, if p were . . . then it would be . . . ; the notion of the "long run," and the notion of verification. The first two pose difficult problems, and it is not surprising that they were frequently neglected and even ignored in the interest of explaining the verification component. It was the notion of verification as satisfactory functioning which was the most distinctively original element in the whole philosophy expounded by James. Consequently he finds it quite difficult to deal with a problem whose solution requires essential reference to verification without allowing the analysis of the latter to become his most important concern. We find, then, comments such as this:

> "Any idea that helps us to deal . . . with either the reality or its belongings, that doesn't entangle our progress in frustrations, that fits, in fact, and adapts our life to the reality's whole setting, will . . . hold true of that reality."[16]

In this extract, no suggestion of the adequacy of mere potential confirmation and no considerations concerning the long run are expressed. On the other hand when he is conscious of the need for meeting formal requirements he is able to combine the first and the second at the same time:

> " *'The true' is only the expedient in the way of our thinking.* . . . Expedient in almost any fashion; and expedient in the long run and on the whole of course; for what meets expediently all the experience in sight won't necessarily meet all future experience equally satisfactorily. Experience has ways of boiling over and making us correct our present formulas."[17]

The third motive suggested, the strong concern for the concrete, was the most important stimulus to James's characterizations of truth in terms of actual rather than potential verification. At the first level of analysis truth is to be conceived as a kind of dispositional property of an "idea":

> . . ."a healthy man need not always be sleeping or always digesting, any more than a wealthy man need always be handling money. . . . All such qualities sink to the status of 'habits' between their times of exercise; and similarly truth becomes a habit of certain of our ideas and beliefs in their intervals of rest from their verifying activities."[18]

. . ."just as a man may be called an heir and treated as one before the executor has divided the estate, so any idea may practically be credited with truth before the verification process has been exhaustively carried out—the existence of the mass of verifying circumstances is enough. Where potentiality counts for actuality in so many cases one does not see why it may not so count here."[19]

As these remarks suggest, a reference to a disposition or a potentiality is always incomplete for James. The disposition-term must be analyzed into the aggregate of concrete events which it denotes. Hence he continues the first remark above by pointing out that nevertheless "those activities [the concrete verifications] are the root of the whole matter, and the conditions of there being any habit to exist in the intervals."

The axiom that a concept is merely an abstraction of a class of concrete particulars and that these particulars exhaust the concept's reference is constantly reiterated. The rule of exposition which is derived from this axiom and equally emphasized in practice is that each abstraction, and hence each concept which one is concerned to understand, should be broken down into its concrete denota. This holds for the concept of truth as well as for any other:

"The pragmatist clings to facts and concreteness, observes truth at its work in particular cases, and generalizes. Truth, for him, becomes a class-name for all sorts of definite working-values in experience."[20]

"The full reality of a truth for him [the pragmatist] is always some process of verification, in which the abstract property of connecting ideas with the objects truly is workingly embodied. Meanwhile it is endlessly serviceable to be able to talk of properties abstractly and apart from their working. . . . We thus form whole universes of platonic ideas *ante rem*, universes *in posse*, though none of them exists effectively except *in rebus*. . . . Countless relations

obtain there which nobody experiences as obtaining. . . .
In the same way countless opinions 'fit' realities, and countless truths are valid, though no thinker thinks them."

"For the anti-pragmatist these prior timeless relations are
the pre-supposition of the concrete ones. . . . When in-
tellectualists do this, pragmatism charges them with invert-
ing the real relations. Truth *in posse* means only truth in
act; and he insists that these latter take precedence in order
of logic as well as in that of being."[21]

Truth is, in the first analysis, a rather abstract relation between
ideas or statements and facts—a relation determining potential
interaction of a certain sort. But there are no abstract relations
in the final analysis, James insists. And since the only concrete
relation which he can find for the prototype of the abstract one
in question, i.e. the verifiability, is that of actual verification, he
reduces the verifiability to a class of concrete verifications. The
result is an oversimplification, but it emanates from a general
theory of abstractions rather than from a theory of truth. The
initial concept of truth remains that of verifiability.

James's great strength, in comparison with Peirce, lies in his
doing justice to concrete particulars. It seems that Peirce's long
run approach to a final verification leaves out the concreteness
of first hand experience that we can undergo only step by step
along the way. Mankind can only live in the present, and though
later historians may approach more closely, in some respects,
than contemporaries to the truth about the present, yet they cannot recover the present that the contemporary experiences at
first hand. James himself was quite conscious that his own
emphasis on the concrete constituted not only the chief difference between him and the others, but also constituted a pregnant
source of misunderstanding on the part of his critics. Referring
to the "anti-pragmatist" in general he writes:

"His trouble seems to me mainly to arise from his fixed inability to understand how a concrete statement can possibly mean as much, or be as valuable, as an abstract one. I said above that the main quarrel between us and our critics was that of concreteness versus abstractness."[22]

And contrasting his view with that of most epistemologists he says:

". . . and the most general way of characterising the two views is by saying that my view describes knowing as it exists concretely, while the other view only describes its results abstractly taken."[23]

Perhaps the best example of a passage in which all three of the motives which have been suggested operate in conjunction with an awareness of the importance of his own nominalism is the following:

"Of course if you take the satisfactoriness concretely . . . and if, by truth, you mean truth taken abstractly and verified in the long run you cannot make them equate, for it is notorious that the temporarily satisfactory is often false. Yet at each and every concrete moment, truth for each man is what the man 'trowth' at the moment with the maximum of satisfaction to himself; and similarly abstract truth, truth verified by the long run, and abstract satisfactoriness, long-run satisfactoriness, coincide. If, in short, we compare concrete with concrete and abstract with abstract, the true and satisfactory do mean the same thing. I suspect that a certain muddling hereabouts is what makes the public so impervious to humanism's claims."[24]

As has already been indicated, Dewey substituted the concept of "warranted assertibility" for that of truth. His analysis of "warranted assertibility" was offered as a definition of the nature of knowledge in the honorific sense according to which only true beliefs are knowledge. If inquiry begins in doubt, it terminates in the institution of conditions which may remove need for doubt. Dewey understands belief as a fitting designation for the outcome of inquiry, and knowledge as a term designating the objective and close of inquiry. Both of these words he finds ambiguous. When it is said that attainment of knowledge, or truth, is the end of inquiry, the statement is a truism, for what satisfactorily terminates inquiry is, by definition, knowledge. But knowledge is sometimes thought to have a meaning of its own apart from connection with and reference to inquiry. The theory of inquiry is then necessarily subordinated to this meaning as what Dewey calls "a fixed eternal end."[25] The idea that knowledge can be instituted apart from its being the consummation of inquiry is one of the sources of confusion in logical theory and has made it subservient to metaphysical and epistemological preconceptions. The general conception of knowledge, when formulated in terms of the outcome of inquiry, has something to say regarding the meaning of inquiry itself. It manifests the "continuing" nature of inquiry, and indicates that the settlement of a particular situation by a particular inquiry is no guarantee that the conclusion will always remain settled. The attainment of settled beliefs is, for Dewey, a progressive matter. There is no belief so settled that it cannot be exposed for further inquiry. When knowledge is taken as a general abstract item related to inquiry in the abstract, it means warranted assertibility.

The most severe attack on Dewey's conception of warranted assertibility has been made by Russell in *An Inquiry into Truth and Meaning* and in the chapter on John Dewey in *A History of Western Philosophy*. Russell thus argues:

"The main difference between Dr. Dewey and me is that he judges a belief by its effects, whereas I judge it by its causes where a past occurrence is concerned. I consider such a belief "true," or as nearly "true" as we can make it, if it has a certain kind of relation (sometimes very complicated) to its causes. . . . This divergence is connected with a difference of outlook on the world. The past cannot be affected by what we do, and therefore, if truth is determined by what has happened, it is independent of present or future violations; it represents in logical form, the limitations of human power. But if truth, or rather "warranted assertibility" depends upon the future, then, insofar as it is in our power to alter the future, it is in our power to alter what should be asserted. . . . If I find the belief that Caesar crossed the Rubicon very distasteful, I need not sit down in dull despair; I can, if I have enough skill and power, arrange a social environment in which the statement that he did not cross the Rubicon will have "warranted assertibility."[26]

Russell's viewpoint is typical of a fairly large section of modern philosophers who have misinterpreted Dewey, albeit in good faith. Thus Russell also comments:

"One important difference between us arises, I think, from the fact that Dr. Dewey is mainly concerned with theories and hypotheses, whereas I am mainly concerned with assertions about particular matters of fact."

But Dewey's viewpoint is surely that something of the order of a theory or a hypothesis, a meaning entertained as a possible significance in some actual case, is demanded, if there is to be warranted assertibility in the case of a particular matter of fact. It is hardly a position that can be put in opposition to assertions about particular matters of fact since it states the conditions only under which we reach warranted assertibility about particular matters of fact.

It is also unfair to ascribe to Dewey, as Russell and other critics have done, the idea that there is an inferential element in all our knowledge. This statement is ambiguous. If it means (as it is apparently intended to mean) that an element due to inference appears in *propria persona,* so to speak, it is incorrect. For according to Dewey's view, while to infer something is necessary if a warranted assertion is to be arrived at, this inferred something never appears, *qua se,* in knowledge. The inferred material has to be checked and tested. The means of testing required to give an inferential element any claim whatsoever to be knowledge instead of conjecture, are the data provided by observation —and only by observation. Moreover, as is stated frequently in *Logic: The Theory of Inquiry,* it is necessary that data (provided by observation) be new, or different from those which first suggested the inferential element, if they are to have any value with respect to attaining knowledge. It is important that they be had under as many different conditions as possible so that data due to differential origins may supplement one another. The necessity of both the distinction and the cooperation of inferential and observational subject-matter is the product of an analysis of scientific inquiry; this necessity is the heart of the whole theory that knowledge is warranted assertion.

Instead of holding that "accepted theories" are always the basis for interpretation of what is newly obtained in perceptual experience, the pragmatist has not been behind others in pointing out that such a mode of interpretation is a common and serious source of wrong conclusions; of dogmatism and of consequent arrest of advance in knowledge. Dewey has explicitly pointed out that one chief reason why the introduction of experimental methods meant such a great change in natural science, is that they provide data which are new not only in detail but in kind. Hence their introduction compelled new kinds of inference to new kinds of subject-matters, and the formation of new types of theories—in addition to providing more exact means of testing old theories.

It is difficult to see how and why, in view of the numerous and oft-repeated statements in Dewey's *Logic* of the necessity for distinguishing between inferential elements and observational data (necessary since otherwise there is no approach to warranted assertibility), it could occur to anyone that he denied the distinction. Perhaps his statements about the necessity of hard data, due to experimental observation and freed from all inferential constituents, were not taken seriously because it was supposed that upon his theory these data themselves represent, or present, cases of knowledge, so that there must be on his theory an inferential element also in them. Whether or not this is the source of the alleged denial thought up by Russell, it may be used to indicate a highly significant difference between the two views. For Russell holds that propositions about these data are in some cases instances of knowledge, and indeed that such cases provide, as basic propositions, the models upon which a theory of truth should be formed. In Dewey's view, they are not cases of knowledge, although propositional formulation of them is a necessary (but not sufficient) condition of knowledge.

The view imputed to Dewey is that "Inquiry uses 'assertions' as its tools, and assertions are 'warranted' insofar as they produce the desired result."[27] I put in contrast with this conception the following statement of Dewey's view:

"Judgment may be identified as the settled outcome of inquiry. It is concerned with the concluding objects that emerge from inquiry in their status of being *conclusive*. Judgment in this sense is distinguished from *propositions*. The content of the latter is intermediate and representative and is carried by symbols; while judgment, as finally made, has *direct* existential import. The terms *affirmation* and *assertion* are employed in current speech interchangeably. But there is a difference, which should have linguistic recognition, between the logical status of intermediate subject-matters that are taken for use in connection *with what they lead to as means,* and subject-matter which has been prepared to be final. I shall use *assertion* to designate the latter logical status and *affirmation* to name the former. . . . However, the important matter is not the words, but the logical properties characteristic of different subject-matters."[28]

Propositions, then on this view, are what are affirmed but not asserted. They are means of instrumentalities, since they are the operational agencies by which beliefs that have adequate grounds for acceptance, are reached as ends of inquiry. The difference between the instrumentality of a proposition as means of attaining a grounded belief and the instrumentality of a belief as means of reaching certain "desired results," should be fairly obvious, independently of acceptance or rejection of Dewey's view.

Unless a critic is willing to entertain, in however hypothetical a fashion, that knowledge in its honorific sense is in every case connected with inquiry; that the conclusion or end of inquiry has to be demarcated from the intermediate means by which inquiry goes forward to a warranted or justified conclusion, and that the intermediate means are formulated in discourse, i.e., as propositions, and that as means they have the properties of relevancy, efficacy and economy appropriate to means, I know of no way to make Dewey's view intelligible. If the view is entertained, even in the most speculative conjectural fashion, it will be clear that according to it, truth and falsity are properties only of that subject-matter which is the end of the inquiry by means of which it is reached. The distinction between true and false conclusions is determined by the character of the operational procedures through which propositions about data and propositions about inferential elements are instituted.

Another passage deserves notice:

"Moreover, inference, even in its connection with test, is not logically final and complete. The heart of the entire theory developed in this work is that the resolution of an indeterminate situation is the end, in the sense in which 'end' means *end-in-view* and in the sense in which it means *close*."[29]

The implication of the passage in its context, is that inquiry begins in an indeterminate situation, and not only begins in it but is controlled by its specific qualitative nature. Inquiry, as the set of operations by which the situation is resolved has to discover and formulate the conditions that describe the problem in hand. For they are the conditions to be "satisfied" and the determinants of "success." Since these conditions are existential, they can be determined only by observational operations; the operational character of observation being clearly exhibited in the experimental character of all scientific determination of data. The conditions discovered, accordingly, in and by operational observation, constitute the conditions of the problem with which further inquiry is engaged; for data, on this view, are always data of some specific problem and hence are not given ready-made to an inquiry but are determined in and by it. As the problem progressively assumes definite shape by means of repeated acts of observation, solutions begin to present themselves. These possible solutions are, truistically (in terms of the theory), possible meanings of the data determined in observation. The process of reasoning is an elaboration of them. When they are checked by reference to observed materials, they constitute the subject-matter of inferential propositions. The latter are means of attaining the goal of knowledge as warranted assertion, not instances or examples of knowledge. They are also operational in nature since they institute new experimental observations whose subject-matter provides both tests for old hypotheses and starting-points for new ones or at least for modifying solutions previously entertained. This procedure continues until a determinate situation is instituted.

When the term "doubtful situation" is taken in the meaning it possesses in the context of his general theory of experience, he means that it can exist without a personal doubter; and, moreover, that "personal states of doubt that are not evoked by, and are not relative to, some existential situation are pathological; when they are extreme they constitute the mania of doubting. . . . The habit of disposing of the doubtful as if it belonged only to us rather than to the existential situation in which we are caught and implicated is an inheritance from subjectivistic psychology."[30] The problematic nature of situations is definitely

stated to have its source and prototype in the condition of imbal-
ance or disequalibration that recurs rhythmically in the interactivity of organism and as a form of organic behavior such as is
manifested, for example, in bodily restlessness and bodily acts
of search for food. All experiences are interactivities of an organism and an environment, and a doubtful or problematic situation is no exception. But the energies of an organism involved
in the particular interactivity that constitutes the problematic
situation are those involved in an ordinary course of living and
are not those of doubting. Doubt can be legitimately imputed to
the organism only in a secondary or derived manner. "Every
such interaction is a temporal process, not a momentary, cross-
sectional occurrence. The situation in which it occurs is indeterminate, therefore, with respect to its *issue*. . . . Even were
existential conditions unqualifiedly determinate in and of themselves, they are indeterminate [are such in certain instances] in
significance: that is, in what they import and portend in their interaction with the organism."[31] This passage should illuminate
the sense in which an existential organism is existentially implicated or involved in a situation as interacting with environing
conditions. According to Dewey's view, the sole way in which a
"normal person" figures is that such a person investigates only
in the actual presence of a problem. All that is necessary upon
his view is that an astronomical or geological epoch be an actual
constituent of some experienced problematic situation.

Though I believe that Dewey's fundamental position is sound,
his exposition raises a number of problems which seem unre-
solved to his critics. In the language of modern symbolic logic,
warranted assertions have truth values whereas propositions
have no truth values. This Deweyan thesis rests on the premise
that because propositions can be regarded as means, they do not
therefore have any truth values. An example will illustrate the
difficulties which some critics see ensuing from this standpoint.
When Galileo was confronted with a number of astronomical
problems to which medieval science gave no answer, he began an

inquiry. This concluded in the assertion that the earth moves round the sun. Let us presume that an admirer of Galileo who had not himself made any such inquiry and had not observed how Galileo had arrived at this result, was going about Florence repeating the same statement that the earth moves round the sun. Galileo's original assertion would have been warranted since it possessed truth value, according to Dewey's theory. The disciple who said word for word the same thing was not, however, making a warranted assertion. He was, at best, stating a proposition since he had not conducted an inquiry; what he was stating was thus, for Dewey, neither true nor false. This means that identical statements may in some cases be true, or false, and in some cases neither, depending on who is speaking.

This difficulty, it seems to me rests on a misinterpretation of Dewey's theory. Surely Dewey would regard the admirer's statement as a warranted assertion if we presume that it has the same meaning as Galileo's assertion. What is essential is not the question of who makes the assertion, but rather what warrants it. Dewey expressly contends that knowledge is not a personal matter. It is, of course, essential to know whether two sentences, word for word the same, have the same meaning. Often they do not. Successful communication requires sameness of meaning, and meaning is much more than a matter of words. But I take it that in this example the meanings of the two statements constitute one connotation. In this light the original problem may appear less formidable.

Since propositions are to be sharply distinguished from warranted assertions, as Dewey insists, it follows again that it is impossible to know whether something is a proposition or warranted assertion unless one has far more than the usually required knowledge of the content of the statement in question. I am in full agreement with his critics on this point. Suppose that at one stage in his inquiry Galileo had affirmed the proposition "the earth moves round the sun." As a proposition this may have had all the characteristics of means in inquiries; it may have

been efficient and fit, but had no truth value. When Galileo concluded his inquiry with the stated assertion "the earth moves
round the sun," he then asserted something which did have
truth value. Thus the two statements differ to this extent: in
spite of apparent identity, one was true or false, the other
neither. It follows, of course, that if one were to deny Galileo's
first statement, or any proposition, the denial would be either
always false or never true or false. For if P is a proposition in
Dewey's sense, the statement "$\sim P$" is itself false since P is
neither false nor true. But our denial of P may not be a product
of inquiry and hence, not being a warranted assertion, it too cannot be true or false. Hence "the earth moves round the sun" and
"the earth does not move round the sun" may both lack truth
values. If neither of these is true or false then they only appear
to be contradictory.

It is not only in the practical areas of communication that
Dewey's theory makes for more stringent demands on our expressions than they may be able to bear. Given some statement
which ordinarily would appear to be asserting something, we
cannot know whether what is being said is assertative at all, i.e.
whether it has any truth value, unless we know if the statement
was produced by inquiry or not. Most of the statements we
make, it would seem, are not "warranted." Yet they do seem to
be assertions about something and their denials do seem to be
genuinely denying something to be the case.

Furthermore, if one regards only statements as having truth
values, as is the custom, then the class of statements shrinks on
this theory to the class of warranted assertions. Statements like
"God is a Trinity of three persons" or "Julius Caesar was sick
on the morning of his seventh birthday" are not true or false for
Dewey since they are not warranted by inquiry. They could
become truth valued if inquiry could render them warranted.
Expressions for which the law of the excluded middle applies are
hence comparatively scarce by the usual standards, since they
alone are warranted assertions. The statements just given, then,

are among the exceptions to this law. These restrictions must be taken into account in considering the merits of Dewey's theory.

Dewey maintains that his "analysis of 'warranted assertibility' is offered as a definition of the nature of knowledge in the honorific sense according to which only *true* beliefs are knowledge."[32] It is almost facile to say that an inquiry that produced an assertion which later turned out to be unwarranted was, strictly, not a genuine inquiry. The assertion then was not really warranted. But this does not mean that "truth and falsity are properties only of that subject-matter which is the *end*, the close of inquiry."[33] It is rather to say that truth is the property of those ends, and that falsity is not a property of inquiry. Warranted assertions, being by definition the warranted products of inquiry, are always true. Any denial or statement appearing to contradict a warranted assertion is not true and hence not true or false. To be true, a denial would have to be warranted, but to be warranted it could not be a denial of something already warranted. The nearest thing such a denial comes to being at all is a proposition and in that case it is neither true nor false. It may seem invidious to emphasize this difficulty but if it constitutes a valid criticism, it would call for a revision of that area of the pragmatic premises.

In conclusion, perhaps some observations on the pragmatic theory of truth in general are apposite. For the pragmatist, truth and falsity depend upon what is found as the result of the careful performance of the experiment of observing reflective events. An empirical finding is refuted not by denial that one finds things to be so and so, but by giving directions for a course of experience that results in finding its opposite to be the case. To convince, of error as well as to lead to truth, consists in assisting oneself and others to see and find something which has hitherto been unrecognized. Though the three philosophers whom I have discussed differ considerably in details, their fundamental premises are to all intents and purposes identical. A good deal of what they have to say is not new and can be found in the writings of earlier philosophers. What is new and significant is their emphasis on the objective universality of meaning and truth as an ideal of logical value to be approximated rather than a factual structure to be claimed. It is this interpretation of the ultimate meaning of all methodological tools which determines the difference between sound and unsound logic.

NOTES

1. Peirce, C. S.: "Collected Papers," Vol. V, Pragmatism and Pragmaticism, Harvard, 1934. § 461.
2. Op. Cit., Vol. V, § 189.
3. Op. Cit., Vol. VI, Scientific Metaphysics, § 490.
4. Op. Cit., Vol. V, § 427.
5. Buchler, J.: "Charles Pierce's Empiricism," Harcourt, Brace and Co., 1939.
6. Op. Cit., p. 155.
7. Peirce, C. S.: Op. Cit., Vol. V, § 430.
8. Op. Cit., Vol. II, § 693.
9. Op. Cit., Vol. VI, § 610.
10. Op. Cit., Vol. V, § 407.
11. James, W.: "Pragmatism," Longmans, 1947. Page numbers are included with the quotations.
12. Perkins, M.: "Notes on the Pragmatist Theory of Truth," *Journal of Philosophy*, Vol. 49, No. 18, Aug. 1952, pp. 573–587.
13. Op. Cit., p. 220.
14. James, W.: "The Meaning of Truth," Longmans, 1909, p. 165.
15. Op. Cit., p. 170.
16. James, W.: "Pragmatism," Longmans, 1947, p. 213.
17. Op. Cit., p. 232.
18. Op. Cit., p. 222.
19. James, W.: "The Meaning of Truth," Longmans, 1909, p. 164.
20. James, W.: "Pragmatism," Longmans, 1947, p. 68.
21. James, W.: "The Meaning of Truth," Longmans, 1909, pp. 203–206.
22. Op. Cit., p. 201.
23. Op. Cit., p. 144.
24. Op. Cit., pp. 88–89.
25. Dewey, J.: "Logic, The Theory of Inquiry," Holt, 1938, p. 8.
26. Russell, B.: "A History of Western Philosophy," Simon and Schuster, 1945.

27. Russell, B.: "An Inquiry into Truth and Meaning," London, 1939, pp. 401–402.
28. Dewey, J.: "Logic, The Theory of Inquiry," Holt, 1938, p. 120.
29. Op. Cit., pp. 157–158.
30. Op. Cit., p. 106.
31. Op. Cit., pp. 106–107. See also by the same author: "Common Sense and Science: Their Respective Frames of Reference," *Journal of Philosophy*, Vol. 45, No. 8, 1948, pp. 197–208.
32. Dewey, J.: "Problems of Men," New York, 1948, p. 332.
33. Op. Cit., p. 340.

List of Symbols

Symbol	Name	Meaning
1. •	Dot	and
2. ∼	Tilde	not
3. v	Wedge	or
4. ⊃	Horseshoe	if . . . then . . .
5. =	Sign of Exact Equivalance	equals
6. ≡	Sign of Material Equiva-lance	if and only if
7. (Ǝ x)	Existential Quantifier	there exists at least one x such that
8. • ⊃ •	Horseshoe between com-plete propositions	if . . . then . . . (with complete propositions.)
9. • = •	Sign of Exact Equivalance between complete pro-positions.	equals (with complete propositions.)
10. • ≡ •	Sign of Material Equiva-lance between complete propositions.	if and only if (with com-plete propositions.)
11. Df	Sign of Definition	by definition
12. ≧	Sign of Qualified Equality	is more than or equal to
13. ≦	Sign of Qualified Equality	is less than or equal to

Index

A TREASURY OF PHILOSOPHY

Edited by Dagobert D. Runes

Here is one of the most comprehensive collections of philosophical writings ever to be gathered between the two covers of one book. In a text of over 1200 pages, under more than 375 separate entries, are to be found, not only the great philosophers of the West, but the important, and less familiar, thinkers of the Orient. The selections cover the whole span of recorded philosophy— from the Sixth Century B.C. to the present day. Each entry begins with a biographical sketch, covering the significant events in the philosopher's life, listing his major works, and including a concise, careful statement of his place and importance in the history of philosophy. This is followed by one or more representative excerpts from the man's work. Depending on the importance of its author, each excerpt runs from a few paragraphs to several pages in length. And each is a self-contained unit of reading matter. Included as a matter of course, are the greater and lesser thinkers of the classic Greek and Roman periods. Added to these are the great Jewish scholars of all periods; the Church Fathers of the Christian Era; the important Oriental teachers, and the whole prodigious line of modern philosophers from the Renaissance to our time.

$15.00